THIS BEAUTY

ALSO BY NICK RIGGLE:

On Being Awesome

THIS BEAUTY

A Philosophy of Being Alive

NICK RIGGLE

BASIC BOOKS
New York

Basic Books
Hachette Book Group
1290 Avenue of the Americas, New York, NY 10104
www.basicbooks.com

Printed in the United States of America

First Edition: December 2022

Published by Basic Books, an imprint of Perseus Books, LLC, a subsidiary of Hachette Book Group, Inc. The Basic Books name and logo is a trademark of the Hachette Book Group.

The Hachette Speakers Bureau provides a wide range of authors for speaking events. To find out more, go to www.hachettespeakersbureau.com or call (866) 376-6591.

The publisher is not responsible for websites (or their content) that are not owned by the publisher.

Print book interior design by Jeff Williams.

Library of Congress Cataloging-in-Publication Data

Names: Riggle, Nick, author.
Title: This beauty : a philosophy of being alive / Nick Riggle.
Description: First edition. | New York, NY : Basic Books, [2022] | Includes
    bibliographical references and index.
Identifiers: LCCN 2022013477 | ISBN 9781541675506 (hardcover) | ISBN
    9781541675513 (ebook)
Subjects: LCSH: Life. | Aesthetics
Classification: LCC BD435 .R54 2022 | DDC 128—dc23/eng/20220808
LC record available at https://lccn.loc.gov/2022013477

ISBNs: 978-1-5416-7550-6 (hardcover), 978-1-5416-7551-3 (e-book)

LSC-C

Printing 1, 2022

To Wolfe

CONTENTS

Chapter 1	The Question	1
Chapter 2	This Life	27
Chapter 3	This Body	63
Chapter 4	This Day	91
Chapter 5	This Time	125
Chapter 6	This Beauty	151
Chapter 7	These People	181
Acknowledgments		215
Index		217

Chapter 1

THE QUESTION

One day I sort of woke up and found myself here. Not here, writing this book, right here and now. But here. In the biggest sense. Here on planet Earth. With a beating heart. With a warm, animate body. Consciousness alight. Time ticking. I had been alive for a while. All of a sudden I was awake.

I didn't ask to be here. I didn't consent to this life. No one spoke with me before all of this to see whether I would mind being a bounded, conscious, material thing thrust into a delicate, short life on some spinning space orb. In some galaxy. In some universe. In some . . . place. Yet here I am.

And there you are.

Hi.

·

I was thirteen years old when I woke up, just finishing the eighth grade, about to enter, and drop out of, high school.

The early years of my life had passed. My dad was an explosive Vietnam War veteran with undiagnosed PTSD. He couldn't keep his cool, struggled to keep his jobs. Mom held an early-morning newspaper route and worked at Domino's Pizza and our church. Neither of them had college degrees. Together, they had four boys.

I knew, from an early age, that I didn't want to spend time in my home, a den of tensions and uncertainties. I spent hours alone in the mysterious backyard, crouching low among crowds of dandelions, eating some, marveling at the blast of acid and waves of saliva—my three-year-old drool a fine distraction from the bursts of anger and confusion inside. Outside, I could mold dirt, build forts, shoot my slingshot, hang with my imaginary friend Van, and lose myself in fantastical tasks and worlds. Inside, there was no hiding from the trembling reality of love trying and failing to shape our nascent family into something coherent, to express its beautiful self—of love bruised by paroxysms of anger and fear.

•

All that time in the backyard, playing guns with neighborhood kids, riding bikes, catching crawdads, going to the Boys & Girls Club, I wasn't just a boy being a boy. I was a boy building a world he could agree to because it was one that he made to his own liking. By age thirteen I had already spent the best part of a decade building and inhabiting my own world.

Then I woke up.

•

I realized that I hadn't agreed to THIS WHOLEASS THING. And I didn't really like where I had ended up. I was still too young to understand that I was, only in a cosmic sense, fucked.

•

A man in India, Raphael Samuel, planned to sue his parents for giving birth to him. He didn't consent to being born, so he figured he deserved lifelong compensation for all the suffering he had, and would have to, endure. His parents, both lawyers, pointed out that if they could have asked him if he wanted to be born, they would have. They couldn't have, obviously, so they aren't to blame for failing to do something they could not have done.

But if you could reasonably expect that your child *would* agree to existence when you *are* able to ask, then would that be agreement enough? You would have to make very sure they'd agree. And with what confidence would you do that?

·

Some think that confidence is assured because life itself is a wonderful gift.

The poem "The Lanyard" by Billy Collins compares a young boy's sincere gift to his mom of a plastic lanyard to the gift of life itself. Parents give us life. They nurse us, love and comfort us. They teach us to walk, swim, talk, and read. They teach us how to eat, how to dress, how to clean up and help out around the house. They introduce us to the world. And in return for this immense gift, little Billy offers his mother the worthless plastic lanyard that he "wove out of boredom" at camp.* The poem ends by offering another gift: the admission that as a boy he was absolutely sure that the useless lanyard would be sufficient repayment for life.

The poem plays with the thought that the gift of life is the most immense, the gift of all gifts, that nothing can repay. The confident offering of a plastic lanyard for life itself exposes the infinite distance between the two, and this exposes the bond, across that distance, between a knowing, loving parent and their precious, innocent child. In this way, the sincere giving of the lanyard is the perfect gift. Anything more would close the gap, and so would be less, and anything less than a plastic lanyard would be nothing.

·

If life is a gift, it is one that requires more giving. Parents also nurture that life, shape it into something, and hopefully offer their child the most

---

* Billy Collins, "The Lanyard," *The Trouble with Poetry and Other Poems* (New York: Random House, 2015), 45–46.

precious gift they can give: some idea of how to live the life they were given.

But the idea that life is a gift given by parent to child is curious. Gifts needn't be repaid. That's the whole idea of a gift. It is gifted.

If life really is a gift, then, you would seem to owe your parents nothing. But, as parents tend to point out, you don't owe them nothing; they expect rather a lot for having given the gift of life—at the very least, that you live your life and make something of it. And if life is not only a gift but such an *immense* gift that it can never be repaid, why expect payment?

From the child's perspective, it becomes very clear very fast that this "gift" comes with several caveats and burdens. And you learn early on that gifts like that aren't very good.

It seems that both parent and child are not entirely comfortable with the thought that life is a gift.

•

Some think that the metaphor of a gift suggests too generous a mode of exchange. Arthur Schopenhauer writes, "Far from bearing the character of a gift, human existence has entirely the character of a contracted debt." But any debt has to be legitimate, and if I did not consent to my existence, then whom or what could I be indebted to? Schopenhauer tries to explain:

> The calling in of this debt appears in the shape of the urgent needs, tormenting desires, and endless misery brought about through that existence. As a rule, the whole lifetime is used for paying off this debt, yet in this way only the interest is cleared off. Repayment of the capital takes place through death. And when was this debt contracted? At the begetting.*

Schopenhauer has a talent for turning what you thought were good things (begettings, music) into bad or strange things (debts, the most direct expression of Will itself). But how is your coming into

---

* Arthur Schopenhauer, *The World as Will and Representation*, vol. 2, trans. E. F. J. Payne, 2nd rev. ed. (New York: Dover, 1968), 580.

existence a debt contracted when nothing in your coming to be can serve as the most essential element of a contracted debt, your agreement? Debts, gifts—metaphors for what you owe for your existence falter.

.

I am becoming a father. As I write this, my wife is pregnant with our first child, a boy. I asked him if he consents to existence, and, despite yelling, DO YOU CONSENT TO EXISTENCE? at my wife's belly, I didn't get a response. He kicks a lot, and we wonder if that means he wants out (in one sense or another).

ME: Hey, fetus, do you consent to existence?
FETUS: Um, are you rich?
ME: No, unfortunately.
FETUS: OK, well, where do you live?
ME: San Diego, California. The weather is perfect, so when you come out, you'll be very pleased, specifically in terms of thermo-comfort.
FETUS: Are you aware of fetal thermo-comfort? It's literally perfect in here. And no one

ever complained about the weather in Nonexistence.

ME: Fair point. You're smart, which will be helpful if/when you exist. Your mom and I are pretty cool and nice, and we'll want to hang out with you all the time and always ask after you and . . . I'm now realizing how this sounds. Well, for the first few years we'll dress, clean, and feed you. You won't have to do a thing.

FETUS: What about after that?

ME: Well, then it's up to you. It would be weird otherwise.

FETUS: Why?

ME: You'll see if/when you exist.

FETUS: The intrigue is unbearable. What about after that?

ME: Well, you'll learn lots of things and meet lots of people and love some of them and eat a lot and grow up and be good and before long you might want to have this exact conversation with your very own fetus.

FETUS: That all sounds very . . . cyclical and odd.

ME: Too bad—it's happening anyway!

I cannot write this book as if I am not becoming a father, as if I won't hand it to my son one day.

·

Why would I want, even slightly, to have consented to my existence? The fact is that I *couldn't have* consented to my existence. I would have had to exist, at least a little, at least as a disembodied consenting mind, in order to consent to existence. But nothing can exist before it exists. So what I want seems impossible to have.

That might make my problem seem incoherent, but to me it just makes it worse. Not only *didn't* I consent, I *couldn't have consented*. And not just as a matter of difficulty. It's impossible. For a moment I thought that might be a relief. "It's impossible to get what you want, so what's the issue? Let it go." But that is no solace to someone who really wants their plight to be different. I also cannot change the past, but I have wanted to. And what is more human than wanting the past to be different? For my family to have been better. To have been more centered and self-reflective. To have held on more tightly to those special people.

To go back and stop my friend from doing that. I want to relive that dinner party, that night, those feelings. But I can't.

•

And *this* is the world I woke up in—*this world, this life, this body, this time, these people, these conditions*. I woke up and found that I can agree and disagree. I consent and contract. I have these special opposable thumbs that go up or down. I have a mouth: it says *yes, please* and *no, thanks* and *let me check my calendar*. I have a motivational mind and a mobile body backing me up and jetting me through worlds of things and thoughts.

I am, at my core, *the very thing I could not be in order to become what I am*. I just had to wake up one day.

•

The weirdest thing is this: even if I could have consented to being alive, what would I have consented to? What the exact fuck *is all of this*? My heart, my tongue, my limbs and thumbs? The Earth? The stars? You? No one *really knows* what this is. It is all one great mystery. However I might imagine my consent, I cannot imagine my informed consent.

Why am I on this orb with feet and a mind rather than disembodied in some ethereal substance or back in the empty nothing whence I came? People run around speaking of gods and spirits and planets and heaven and hell, but as far as I can tell, they don't really know what they are talking about. I wish they did. I wish I had some good and clear and definitive answer.

But they just remind me of my younger self in my backyard, running away, building fantastical worlds when they're too scared or alienated or puzzled or betrayed by the one they are really in.

I did not agree to any of this, and I don't know what the fuck it is anyway. That's the predicament I am in.

You are too.

Hi again.

.

Why should I care about or value this thing that I simply find myself with, this life that was simply given to me, *as me*, even if it is valuable?

If someone randomly walks up to me and hands me a plain old rock, I don't think for a second that I should care about it. I might admire the whimsy of the person who did that or wonder about their sanity. But goodbye, rock. Now suppose that they handed me something everyone agrees is valuable—say, the keys to a Ferrari. Why should I value it? I don't mean: why should I judge, along with everyone else, that it is good? I mean: why should I *want* it, *love* it, *care* for it, make it *mine*? Not because it is indeed very valuable. It is not true that I should value everything that is very valuable. Assuming there are many such things, caring for all of them is impossible. And what if I don't want a Ferrari? The Ferrari was imposed on me. I didn't ask for a Ferrari, and owning one is, yeah, maybe fun, but a pricey hell of a burden. You have to learn how to drive it; it's extremely delicate and finicky, has a rocky suspension, needs a garage, regular tuning, frequent cleaning; and it garners way too much attention—dumb jokes, requests to take a picture, every tricked-out Subaru revving its engine at the red light.

•

I didn't ask to be here, I didn't consent to being alive. One day I woke up and found myself here. And so what? Why should I value this life that I simply find myself with?

This question, this thought—I think of it as *The Question*—is not about death or suicide. Nor is it about the many other ills that plague us: the climate disaster, the death of the planet, literal plagues, the potential end of humanity due to global war or famine, gratuitous pain and suffering in children, natural disasters, systemic injustice, cancer, oppression, and so on.

The Question arises prior to those concerns. It is about *birth*, about coming to be the kind of thing I am, in the kind of world I am in. To me, the most puzzling thing about being alive is not that one day I won't be—that I will die, we will die, everything will die and end up nowhere, as nothing, just as before—but rather that I came from nothing and know fundamentally nothing about where or what I am. And yet I am told that life is worth living. The day is worth seizing, the moment worth embracing. *You only live once.* So what?

If I could answer The Question, then many questions I have about death would fall away. When I know the answer, then I will know that I should do this or that. One day I will die. And then, just as before, I'll do nothing, become nothing.

To be aware of, and to love, being what I am—an embodied, thoughtful, conscious being for whom understanding and agreement are everything but, at the beginning, nothing—that is the situation I need to confront, the feeling I have to address. It is not the feeling that death haunts me or calls my life into question. It is not the worry that I will be kidnapped *into nothing*. It is the feeling of having been abducted *from nowhere*.

•

Is there an answer to The Question? If there is, that answer will not come in the form of some story about the cosmos and gods, or about some heaven or hell that awaits me when my life is over. It will come, if at all, in the form of an idea about how being alive can justify itself despite this strange and basic predicament that you and I are in. If I could somehow feel that I belong here, deeply, importantly, repeatedly, not even certainly—if I could feel at home in this life and own that feeling, cultivate it, repeat and propagate it—then I could love this life and not merely live it out.

What could do that? That is what this book is about.

•

You and I—we are delicate. We are flesh. We attract dirt. We sweat and stink. We can burn and boil. We are puncturable, destructible, crushable, explodable. Being so close to death means death can easily nudge us into its arms in the form of a strong wind, a small bacterium, a dumb mistake. Weak and omnipresent gravity draws everything into itself, from a Kleenex to an entire culture.

I have known this my whole life, from the series of fat lips I had throughout childhood, from so many misadventures, scabs, and bruises. If there was a tree, I was in it, seeing and ignoring the hint of death in the allure of the highest branches. If there was something I could jump off, I did. Learning to ride a bike was learning to bunny-hop, wheelie, skid, and fly headfirst over the handlebars. Between the ages of fifteen and twenty-one, I was a professional skater, my body littered with scabs, fractures, stitches, concussions, and contusions.

From the moment you were born, you lived on the brink of easy destruction. There is so much that must happen, and then so much you must do, to keep your little heart beating, to maintain homeostasis, to preserve your fleshy body and keep the blood flowing.

And yet *this* is not the thought that tends to occur to me when, in a certain mood, I think about my one and only life, or about my day as I wake up and it stretches out before me, or about this very moment, or about my living, breathing body as I feel my heart beating softly and regularly. I do not think about preserving my delicate, precious life. Quite the opposite: I think of launching myself into life. I think of boldness, experimentation, adventure, and spontaneity. There are times when the value of being alive seems to jump out and speak to me, in different moments, different registers: I might be moved by thinking of my life as a whole, or in the context of a single day, or of this exact moment.

Why? If I am this delicate and precious being, if life is so fleeting and limited, the moment so elusive—why shouldn't I protect and preserve the one precarious and shining thing I was unwittingly given? There is only one precious, irreplaceable, playable Stradivarius guitar in the world. Nobody plays it.

Yet the thought that *you only live once* does not move me to *preserve* the one delicate life I have. I don't feel the impulse to protect and preserve my beating heart. I want it to beat faster. I want it to beat harder, wilder. And I know I'm not alone.

The thought that you only live once hints at an answer to The Question. I want to know why this life I have been unwittingly given is not only good but *worth my engaging with its goodness*. Worth embracing it, loving it, amplifying it, repeating it. I experience glimmers of an answer through the media of lived life: in the feel of a moment, in the cadence of a good day, the rush of inspiration, the recognition of beauty, the love of my family, the bonds of my community. I think that the day must be seized, the moment embraced, the body adored—you only live once and this is it.

These are things many people tell themselves and each other in affirmation of their lives. These clichés are printed on throwaway coffee mugs, dreadful wall art, styleless T-shirts, and every other book on Amazon.com. *Live like there's no tomorrow. YOLO: you only live once. Seize the day. Get the most out of life. Live in the moment.* What does it mean to "seize the day," to "live like there is no tomorrow," to "live in the moment," or to be moved by the thought that you only live once?

These phrases are "existential imperatives" that direct you to embrace life in certain ways. But whatever promise they might seem to possess is tempered by the strangeness that appears as soon as you put a little pressure on them. Despite their power, prevalence, and social and cultural importance, they are puzzling. In fact, a little scrutiny shows that they are *conceptually odd*, *ethically problematic*, and *logically incoherent*.

Consider *live like there's no tomorrow.*

Why should you live like there's no tomorrow? Why isn't that terrible, irresponsible advice? It might have you saying things you shouldn't, selling beloved goods, or swinging from a chandelier, living like tomorrow doesn't exist. Like it doesn't exist! But it does. If you survive the chandelier escapade, you will have to clean up after yourself. And how should you follow the advice to live as if there is no tomorrow? I know how to act when I'm pretending to be Sia on a karaoke stage. But pretending there's no tomorrow? What is that supposed to inspire in me? You might think that if there were no tomorrow, then you should seize the day. Make the most of it. Live for now. But what does any of that mean? Are you seizing the day if you eat a healthy and complete breakfast and have a great day at work? Or do you have to eat ten tacos and tell your boss to fuck off? And why should you seize the day, anyway? Because you only live once! So what? Well, today might be your last day on earth! It probably won't be, but just imagine that it is!

Similar problems arise with the other existential imperatives. So why is anyone drawn to them? Why do people use these phrases, and why, despite their glaring problems, are they effective? These questions are philosophically pressing. It is so easy to invest inspiration and a sense of life's meaning in the values and ideals that these phrases so easily evoke. They seem to inspire *despite* their oddity and incoherence. And even if you cringe at every utterance of "YOLO," as you probably should, that does not make you immune to its spirit, which can affect you unexpectedly and in a number of ways.

If I could answer the question of how existential imperatives work, why they inspire an embrace of life, then I might have some answer to The Question. Even if I wouldn't use them often myself, I might be assured that there is something to them after all, some truth about being alive that they tap into.

•

I don't know how many ways there are of answering The Question, but I do know that I found an answer that I love. In what follows I want to lead you to it. I want to justify, so I can repeat, the poet and novelist Ocean Vuong's thought. The narrator writes to his abusive mother,

> It is no accident, Ma, that the comma resembles a fetus—that curve of continuation. We were all once inside our mothers, saying, with our entire curved and silent selves, more, more, more. I want to insist that our being alive is beautiful

enough to be worthy of replication. And so what? So what if all I ever made of my life was more of it?*

This life is troubling and trying, but what if you could show that it is beautiful enough to "replicate"? You replicate life *as beautiful* when you engage with, create, and respond to life's beauty with your own beauty, through your ways of interacting with others, through your own products, interpretations, and insights, in the subtle and significant ways you cast your aesthetic attention and act on what it sees.

If being alive is beautiful enough to be worthy of replication, then I can live my life attending to and replicating its beauty, while you do the same. We each do this for ourselves and for one another, in recognition of our each needing to feel connected

---

* Ocean Vuong, *On Earth We Are Briefly Gorgeous* (New York: Penguin Press, 2019), 139. Vuong's beautiful passage at pp. 138–139 appears to be influenced by Plato's *Symposium*, written around 385 BC (see the version translated by Alexander Nehamas and Paul Woodruff [Indianapolis, IN: Hackett, 1989]), and Elaine Scarry's *On Beauty and Being Just* (Princeton, NJ: Princeton University Press, 1999).

to this life, to have a home here. And why wouldn't that be enough to answer The Question? I did not consent to this life, no one had a chat with me to see if I wouldn't mind being here a while—but come take part in this beauty. Come see it, grasp it, create it, share it. You and I are among this. We make this. Maybe we *are* this. In spite of everything, there is a beauty that propels me through life, hoping to create more of it and offer it up to you so you can do the same. Cyclical, perhaps, but not odd, my son.

Vuong writes of *wanting to insist*. I know that desire, and sometimes it seems that all you can do is insist on the beauty of life. I do want to insist. But I feel the need to understand this desire, and as much as I might want to, I cannot insist on something I don't understand. What if I could prove it? Or at least prove the worth of the wanting, of the insisting?

Any proof will come from reimagining beauty. The beautiful or the aesthetic—I use these terms interchangeably here—is not some pretty face or silky sky. Some people think of beauty as the antiquated partner in crime of the so-called fine arts, some associate it with flowers and nice faces. Think of the word here as the literary form of the more

academic "aesthetic value," which is restricted neither to art nor to the flowery and fragrant but is
broader than both: it includes sneakers, design,
decor, fashion, rap, literature, punk, adventure,
play, the wild, the shocking, the challenging, dope-
ness, sleekness, silliness, and style. If life is beautiful
enough to be worthy of replication—if this beauty
can address The Question—then what this beauty
will move you to do, the form of life it will justify repeating, will not be some private ecstasy or
a movement toward a fleeting attraction. It will be
something bigger than you or me. Beauty is an invitation and acceptance, a joint enterprise, if not a
promise of happiness then a promise to give each
other our best answers to The Question.

Throughout this book I imagine a reader,
"you," just as you, when you read it, imagine an
author, "me." To help you along, I offer you pieces
of my life throughout. But I can only imagine you.
I hope you don't mind, but I *have* imagined you. I
have imagined bringing you up. You are my son.
You are not my son. When you imagine me, imagine me thinking that you are thoughtful and good,
that you are someone I can talk with about new

ideas and the way I want to develop them, my ways of thinking that might be your ways too. You are here now, listening, thinking, and imagining. In our exchange—of the author, me, imagining "you" as I have done, and you imagining "me" as I hope you will—we engage in a way of interacting that is at the heart of this book.

The thoughts here come from decades of loving thinking, from having found a place, for me a refuge and home, in thought. I am a philosopher who works with ways of understanding and imagining the world. Here I develop some ideas, consider some claims and arguments, play with thoughts, perspectives, and concepts. I lay them down, juxtapose them, spin them around in the hopes that you will see through them differently and maybe see your life in a certain light, one that is beautiful. Play is one of the concepts I offer up, along with beauty and aesthetic value, home, invitation, individuality, expression, gift, sharing, community, freedom, and love. I use these concepts to light up this life, this body, this day, this time, this beauty, us. I layer and fit them together here and give this to you.

Chapter 2

THIS LIFE

This is your life—the only one you will ever have and the one that, when it is gone, will be absolutely gone forever. Time, earth, raw force: they will conspire to reduce, disintegrate, and scatter your body, as they did the bodies of your ancestors and will the bodies of your descendants, obliterating all trace of your being, returning it to the uncanny nothingness from which we all mysteriously emerged. This is your life. The only one you will ever have. When it is gone, it will be absolutely gone forever.

The idea that *you only live once* has, for better and worse, long influenced humanity. In the opening scene of Goethe's early play *Clavigo* (1774),

Carlos uses it to justify ambitious social climbing: "It seems to me . . . that one lives only once in this world, has only once this power, these prospects, and he who does not make the most of them, and rise as high as possible, is a fool." * The embedded clause is remarkable: *and rise as high as possible.* The claim is not that he who does not make the most of life is a fool. You live only once, Carlos believes, so do whatever you can to increase your standing in a cruel and arbitrary class system. Goethe's line inspired the composer Johann Strauss II for his waltz "Man lebt nur einmal!" which is basically German for YOLO. Over one hundred years later, ABC's abysmal soap opera *One Life to Live* aired, and it ran for forty-three years, from 1968 to 2012. It included several plotlines involving people apparently coming back from the dead.

---

* Perhaps in the spirit of YOLO, Goethe wrote the play in a week. It was published two months later and performed a month after that. No one liked it. See Rüdiger Safranski, *Goethe: Life as a Work of Art*, trans. David Dollenmayer (New York: Liveright), 141. Johann Wolfgang Von Goethe, *Early Verse Drama and Prose Plays* (Goethe: The Collected Works, vol. 7), eds. Cyrus Hamlin and Frank Glessner Ryder (Princeton: Princeton University Press, 1994).

More recently and vociferously, people announce their embrace of life with "YOLO," the hashtagable acronym for "you only live once." YOLO is impressively annoying in both content and form, and everyone who doesn't love it loves to hate it. Even Drake, who is credited with coining the term in his song "The Motto," appears to regret his part in popularizing it: "I sincerely apologize," he said in an opening monologue for *Saturday Night Live.* "I did not know your annoying friends and coworkers would use it so much." Urban Dictionary's top definitions of "YOLO" include, in addition to "The douchebag's mating call," "The dumbass's excuse for something stupid that they did."

The connection between *you only live once* and being adventurous, unusual, or taking risks is familiar, but it resonates in the twenty-first century. Applicants to the Tufts University class of 2018 were asked to write short essay responses to various prompts. Among them was the following:

The ancient Romans started it when they coined the phrase "Carpe diem." Jonathan Larson proclaimed "No day but today!" and most recently,

Drake explained You Only Live Once (YOLO). Have you ever seized the day? Lived like there was no tomorrow? Or perhaps you plan to shout YOLO while jumping into something in the future. What does #YOLO mean to you? ✶

Recent trends take *you only live once* far beyond waltzing, social climbing, and even soap-operatic drama to next-level absurdity and danger. On September 2, 2012, the rapper Ervin McKinness, aka Inkyy, aka Jew'elz, tweeted this: "Drunk af going 120 drifting corners #FuckIt YOLO." Minutes later, the car he was in ran a red light and crashed into a wall. He died along with the other four people in the car.[*]

Why is *you only live once* so persistent across, and distorted by, time and culture? You only live once, so take the plunge, quit your bullshit job, try new and thrilling things, go out and experience the world, *rise as high as possible.*

---

[*] CBSNews.com, "Southern California rapper tweets YOLO, then dies in a suspected drunk-driving crash, reports say," CBS News, September 11, 2012, www.cbsnews.com/news/southern -california-rapper-tweets-yolo-then-dies-in-a-suspected-drunk -driving-crash-reports-say/.

·

When you separate *you only live once* from the extremes and idiocies, you are left with a thought that really does seem intimately related to the love of life. Simple reflection on your one and only life can be enough to send you frenzied into the uncertain world, embracing life with greater freedom and receptivity.

Right now you can pause and observe your surroundings, sense your body, stare at your hands holding this book. You can slow down and feel your heart beat from the inside. There are sounds you hadn't noticed. The wind, the hum of your home. The rustling around you. Your breath.

This is it. *This* is your life. Absolutely everything you are seems to be with you here, now. This is your one and only life. This moment. It is gone. Now this moment. And this. Now gone. Forever.

Now.

Now.

Sounds soften, light intensifies, your body warm with teeming blood is real, present. Your birth and death—mere abstractions just a moment ago, part of some vague background story—now seem somehow simultaneously present and absent as some ghostly structure attending your breath and surroundings, bracketing each moment, suspending you in the strange ether of *now*, of life as it arises and vanishes.

Before this pause and softening, your life was framed by your concrete plans and everyday concerns—you carved out time to sit down and read this book, you thought about your day, your week. Exercise, dinner plans, work. You read the first several pages, and you thought about your own past: your family then, your little self. And, inevitably, this put you in mind of an articulated future, projected from the outline of your everyday life. Your birth was the hazy beginning of a long story, your death an abstract and distant end. Hopes, fears, aspirations, disappointments, struggles—all sprinkled throughout.

Now the vibrancy of your life in this very moment is salient, and a more urgent sense of time stretches out before you. It is clearer now: the life you received unbidden is good, worth seizing, loving, embracing, throwing mightily into the world, into an open future.

•

When you think *you only live once,* a spirit rushes in and transfigures your core, some urgent world springs into focus, and you want to receive it, embrace it, launch yourself into it. Into the wild and unknown, into the beautiful and large, into uncertainty and adventure.

This experience is not just a feeling. It seems to contain a whole way of being. Is this what freedom fundamentally is, to be able to embrace and act from this state of mind? This experience seems to contain some kind of answer to The Question. Or, rather, to hint that The Question *has* an answer, that I have access to a way of being that can confront The Question. True, I did not consent to this whole thing, this mysterious and troubled existence, but when I zero in with attention and care, I am overwhelmed: *This. This is good.* I don't feel lucky, I don't feel grateful, I don't suddenly think that my life is a gift. I am simply amazed, free, moved, and free of The Question. I want to become this amazement. I want it to legislate my life.

•

You only live once is a phrase that turns on two elements: life and its extremely limited supply.

Having only one of this valuable thing makes you think that you should relate to it in a certain way. So maybe the magic lies in this: when you have only one of something, especially something valuable, then you should use that thing. Use it properly, the way it deserves to be used. You have only one life, so *do something* with it.

I have only one guitar. I bought it with the last of the money I made as a professional skater (the rest I put toward college). I played it nearly every day, often for hours, well into my twenties. I learned and wrote scores of songs on it. I used it to record an album as the lead singer in a band (a folk-meets-hip-hop band; it was the early 2000s), and it was onstage with me for many shows. The abstract, fading tattoo on the back of my left shoulder is a partial outline of this guitar. But these days, some twenty years later, I hardly play it. I pick it up now and then and mess around. It mostly sits in my office at home collecting dust. I look at it and remember everything it gave me. I know I should play my precious guitar more, but is that because I have only one?

There are so many things I have only one of: a can opener, a car, my left pinkie finger, a pair of hiking boots, a bread machine. Human beings have been making bread for as many as thirty thousand years, but thanks, I guess, to the groundbreaking 1986 Raku Raku Pan Da electronic bread maker, you can have a machine do most of the work in your very own home. You put some dough mixture into it, press start, and get a loaf of bread in a few hours. It is strange and amazing, and I never use it. But I don't really care. I like making bread the old-fashioned way. The thought that I have only one bread machine does not move me at all. It's the same for my left pinkie, my can opener, and my hiking boots: I'll use them because I want to, not because they are singular.

So there seems to be no *general* connection between having only one of something valuable and putting that thing to use. But the problem is even worse. Suppose that having one bread machine did mean that I should do something with it: why should I use it *as a bread maker* rather than as a step stool? The thought that you only live once does not just tell you to do something with your life— it tells you to live it *in a particular way*. The idea isn't that you should be risky every once in a while or that you should give vitality and verve a try. It is that you should be a certain kind of person, with a certain sensibility and style, one who embraces life, who is open to the world, who is comfortable with adventure and uncertainty. But having one bread machine does not mean I should use it at all, let alone become an expert in making adventurous, risky, or extraordinary loaves of bread.

Whatever the connection is between having one life and embracing life, it must be more particular than having only one of something valuable: having only one *bread machine* gives me no connection to a bread-embracing thought. But having only one *life. That* matters. When you have only one *of those*, then you should embrace it in all of its precarious glory. For this to work, life must be special in some way.

But this is essentially the issue I am pursuing here, The Question, or at least one of its close cousins. When I am in the grip of The Question, I am not so sure that my life is special. Or, at least, I would like to understand why it is something I should care about or live in one way rather than another. But even if I take as a given that life is special, I want to prove and not merely insist that it is special in the right way, in a way that answers The Question.

The problem is that life seems special in exactly the wrong way to answer The Question. The most immediate way that life is special is that it is *precious*, *shockingly fleeting*, and *utterly delicate*. As such, it seems like *you only live once* should inspire the preservation of this wonderfully special thing. I want to understand the power of *you only live once* to understand why life is special. But when I contemplate how special it seems, the impulse to embrace life slips further away.

Another way to put this: why isn't *you only live once* used to inspire the exact *opposite* thought? If life is so precious and you have only one, then you should be a hypochondriac, extremely risk-averse, and at least mildly agoraphobic. You only live once, after all, so don't take any risks. In fact, be *extra* careful.

Slight chance of lightning? Totally staying in tonight. #YOLO

I'll take a burger, extra well done, please. #YOLO

Would shake your hand but #YOLO

Precisely this idea—that YOLO can seem to motivate the extreme opposite of adventure and risk—animates a 2013 *Saturday Night Live* "digital short" music video by the Lonely Island (Andy Samberg, Akiva Schaffer, and Jorma Taccone) featuring Adam Levine and Kendrick Lamar. The song transforms "YOLO" from the risk-inspiring acronym to the risk-averse *you oughta look out*. Life is precious, rare, and under constant threat. Put that on a mug.

Let's call this *the Preservationist Objection*:

The thought that you only live once motivates the exact opposite of adventure, spontaneity, and risk. Your life is precious, fragile, and unique. If you only live once, then you should protect and preserve the one precious thing you have.

The Preservationist is anyone who thinks that life itself, biological human life, is the most precious thing one has, to be preserved at all cost. Or anyone who thinks that *keeping oneself alive*, keeping one's heart beating in decent health, is enough to answer The Question, to make life worth living. Who are the actual Preservationists? They are everywhere. Me? Me in certain moods? You?

If the Preservationist Objection is right, then *you only live once* does not motivate or justify life-embracing actions. Doing so is not only irrational but deeply confused: such things only threaten the one thing that makes life worth living—life itself. To understand the power of *you only live once*, then, the Preservationist needs answering.

•

A natural thought is that you only live once works by reminding you of death. The fact that you only live once, combined with the fact that you are not immortal, means that you are guaranteed a very final ending. And, rightly or not, the contemplation of death is one of the more time-honored ways to put your life in perspective.

But if *you only live once* stokes the thought of death, then why should it move you to do things that have a nontrivial chance of *causing* your death? The contemplation of death plays right into the Preservationist's hand. You only live once! Which means you will die! You oughta look out.

One answer might be that a YOLO death is somehow preferable to a non-YOLO death. But I don't see how an extraordinary death is better than a boring, everyday dusty one. I'm pretty sure I would rather die old and in my sleep than splattered on a mountainside in a squirrel suit. Though I do see the appeal of the latter (supposing the timing is right).

You only live once might put you in vague mind of your death, but if you think about it carefully, you will notice that the reflections inspired by death are not quite the same as those inspired by your one and only life. Death is immense, and contemplating it can put you in mind of any number of things—of what you have done here and what you will leave behind, of your loved ones, of the future of humanity. You might think of what you haven't done or never will do. You can respond to these thoughts in so many ways: with regret, despair, frustration, or, if you are lucky, acceptance or even contentment. In contemplating death, you might be motivated to change, to live more resolutely, or wildly, or authentically, but the thought of death alone does not inspire that. Life does—the thought that you still have a chance to do something.

If there is a connection between death and *you only live once*, then it is not straightforward. Perhaps the connection is mediated by the idea that your life can be meaningful: *you only live once*, which means you will die, so make it count. Find meaning wherever you can: in wild adventure, soaring fun, or bold commitment. To make this work, there must be a connection between meaning and death. And whatever that connection is, it cannot play into the hands of the Preservationist, since for them, it is obvious that death makes life meaningful—their entire ethos is the avoidance of death.

According to the influential British philosopher Bernard Williams (1929–2003), "Death gives the meaning to life." * Williams has a clever way of arguing for this claim. He argues that if you were *immortal*, then your life would be meaningless. The logical contrapositive of this claim is that for your life to have meaning, you have to die. Death is

---

* Bernard Williams, "The Makropulos case: Reflections on the tedium of immortality," in *Problems of the Self: Philosophical Papers 1956–1972* (Cambridge, UK: Cambridge University Press, 1973), 82–100.

necessary for a meaningful life. It "gives the meaning to life."

Why think that living forever would drain life of meaning? Because, Williams argues, living forever would be *extremely boring*. You live in pursuit of your interests, and some of those interests make your life worth living: you wake up at 4 a.m., before the baby, to write books; you work sixteen-hour days to cure cancer; you try to create a more just legal system; you work tirelessly to study for the exam; or you strive to create and play music. Pursuing these things makes your life meaningful in philosopher Susan Wolf's sense: it engages you in projects and practices that wed fulfillment to genuine worth.* They are also what make you interesting *to yourself*: you don't brag about satisfying your desire to eat lunch and pee; on a first date, you don't discuss your fascinating desire to stay relatively dry. Of course you also want these simpler things, but you don't stay alive for them. You stay alive to make art, cure cancer, better the world, see your children have children.

---

* Susan Wolf, *Meaning in Life and Why It Matters* (Princeton, NJ: Princeton University Press, 2010).

To satisfy these desires, you might even ignore simpler desires: lose sleep, go hungry, wait in the rain, ignore the electric bill, or even put your life in serious danger if necessary to save your children or test the vaccine.

Williams thinks that immortality would eat away at the projects that give your life meaning. Cancer would be cured or be proven incurable; you would be an n-teenth great-grandparent, bored with yet another batch of offspring. Immortality would allow you to achieve *all* of your meaningful goals, and the more you succeed, the more your sense of meaning and self will diminish. When you satisfy them all, your sense of self will disappear, and you will no longer know what to live for because there will be nothing left. And that is the definition of boredom.

So if Williams is right, then there is a connection between death and meaning. If death makes life meaningful, then perhaps reflecting on death can be a way of reflecting on life's meaning. *You only live once* could be the lively mediator, allowing you to tap in to certain aspects of life's meaning and moving you to pursue them even at the risk of pain, discomfort, challenge, and suffering.

Perhaps *you only live once* could work this way, but that would not fully capture its power. Death might put you in mind of your meaningful projects—*finish the book, travel to Rome, learn Spanish*—but *you only live once* is even more powerful than that: it can move you to adopt *new* meaningful projects, abandon old ones, and transform your life. Thinking *you only live once* might move you to become a different person. *You only live once* reaches well beyond meaning into the wilderness.

Furthermore, the Preservationist can happily make the point that the preservation of life itself might be meaningful enough—pee when you have to pee, cozy up when you're cold, eat when hunger calls, grab a drink after work with a colleague. Maybe that would be a little boring, but boredom alone is no deterrent to the Preservationist, whom you can imagine being proudly risk-averse and comfortably bored. Only *extreme* or *despairing* boredom would threaten their existence. And if there is anything to do to keep immortal life going—food, sleep, sex, baths, massages, socializing, drying off—then they will simply, happily do that forever. That's the difficulty with the Preservationist:

to them, even immortal life could be meaningful enough.

A deeper problem arises even if *you only live once* works only by putting you in mind of your meaningful projects. The enthusiasms of *you only live once* can and do engage you in your life projects; it can inspire you to try harder, work longer, reconnect. The phrase is not limited to inspiring death-defying Superman stunts. Thinking *you only live once* makes me wonder why I don't play guitar much anymore. Am I forgetting something? Am I not understanding some important lesson? Will I end up wishing on my deathbed that I had devoted more of my life to music?

There were times in my early twenties when nothing made me feel more alive than playing guitar—singing with friends, writing songs, playing shows with the band. I felt that there couldn't be anything better to do with my life—with *a* life— than that. Sometimes when I look at my dusty guitar, I wonder if I let something important die in me. What did I lose my grip on? Why don't I spend time writing, singing, playing music? I don't know.

Maybe it's because I'm busy writing things like this. I suppose that, when all is said and reckoned, I care more about written words than anything sung or strummed. But, as devoted as I am to writing, that fact saddens me. If you could experience the force with which my younger self envisioned a lifetime of musical love, then you'd be a little sad too. It's a sadness that makes me want to embrace life and pick up my guitar. It's almost as if I want two lives, equally in love with words and music.

The fact that I can't—I am limited; I will die—turns my sadness into frustration, and reflecting on that frustration does not make me want to embrace life. This finitude, this limitation, makes life seem too big for this little world, as if life is such that I can't *live only once*, as much as that phrase makes me want to, which makes my motivation for living seem as if it can't fully deliver what it demands. The English literary critic and poet William Empson was right: there is more in the child than anyone has been able to keep.

•

So maybe what mediates between death and *you only live once* is the opposite thought, not that life is meaningful but that it is, in a sense, meaningless or absurd.

The thought of death reminds me that I am but the speckiest of specks on a speck of a planet in one specky galaxy among many billions. The octopus has been around for over three hundred million years, civilized *Homo sapiens* for a mere five thousand. And it is taking us a mere two hundred or so to destroy all the octopuses (and everything else).

What's the point of it all? Life is absurd. When I zoom out and take a bird's-eye or cosmic perspective on my life, I lose my grip on the thought that I should care at all. I begin to doubt the seriousness with which I tend to regard my life. Think of your life as the blip that it is, over so soon, spent doing more or less ordinary things. You are one fleshy blob among many, in an instant of time, in the void of space. The perspective reveals an almost comical gap between the urgent importance you attach to your life and the utter nothing that your life will amount to no matter what you do.

And yet you are like me: you continue to act as if what you do matters. I worry about not playing guitar; I wonder if I ought to use my bread machine; I wake up very early to have time to write; I think that I should love my one and only life. The fact that I continue in this way despite my cosmic insignificance is absurd.* To use an example from Thomas Nagel as modified by J. David Velleman, it's as if my pants fall down as I am being knighted, and I remain utterly poised for the ceremony, pants around my ankles, proud of the honor I seem not to deserve.**

But come to think of it, isn't that the most YOLO thing to do? To own and embrace such an unpredictable moment?

Pants totally fell down as I was being knight-ed. Didn't lose eye contact with the King. #medievalAF #thoudostlivestonlyonce

Such a response seems like the kind of thing that might be inspired by *you only live once*. Life is indeed short; you are indeed a blobby blip. Can't let a faulty belt stop you from being enno-bled. The bird's-eye or cosmic perspective that so

---

* This understanding of life's absurdity is developed by Thomas Nagel in "The Absurd" in *Mortal Questions* (Cambridge, UK: Cambridge University Press, 1979), 11–23.

** J. David Velleman, "Life Absurd? Don't Be Ridiculous" in *Foundations for Moral Relativism* (Cambridge, UK: Open Book Publishers, 2013), 89–97.

easily casts doubt on the seriousness with which you tend to live your life can also move you to embrace it.

Nagel seems to overlook this possibility when he recommends an ironic attitude in response to life's absurdity. He points out that if life is absurd and nothing *really* matters, then the fact that nothing matters *also* does not matter. So why worry? Instead, "we can approach our absurd lives with irony instead of heroism or despair" (1971, p. 727). Nagel recommends irony because life turns out to be exactly what we expect it not to be—your life seems so monumental, so utterly important. And yet, from the cosmic perspective, your life ain't shit. You simply have to live with these two irreconcilable perspectives, and since it doesn't really matter anyway, you should not be too committed to either one. Better to live at an ironic distance from each. It's as if your pants fall down while you are being knighted, and no matter what you do, you cannot pull them up, you can't hide away, and, with your pants down, you also can't act like a fully dignified knight. You just have to be down to walk around like that, head held high, ready with a knowing smirk and a shrug.

I am all for laughter, but irony is not love. The very perspective that might alienate you from your life by showing you that you take it too seriously can also inspire an embrace of life when it impresses you with the thought that *you only live once*. I won't opt for distance and detachment when there is a promise of embrace lurking behind existential imperatives.

.

So why does *you only live once* inspire an embrace of life rather than the attitudes and responses associated with the feeling that life is absurd—existential despair, alienation, or ironic detachment? Maybe Friedrich Nietzsche has an answer. By all accounts, he appears to be the nineteenth century's preeminent YOLOer. And he is sort of a nihilist who thinks that life is absurd, in a sense. But that doesn't stop him from thinking that you should make every effort to embrace or "affirm" life.

Nietzsche firmly believes that you only live once and that it is important to take this seriously. But in a clever move, he evokes *you only live once* vibes by combining the idea of eternal life with the idea of life on Earth. He has you imagine that you have only one *type* of life that you live over and over again. So you have infinitely many lives, but they all have the same character or description—you do exactly the same thing in each life. If you're a grocery store clerk in one, you're a clerk in all; if you're a parent in one, you're a parent in all; if you are a knight in one, you're a knight in all, pants falling down to infinity.

Nietzsche thinks that if you imagine the "eternal recurrence" (as he calls it) of your life vividly enough, then you will be moved to adopt an embracing attitude toward life. He asks,

What, if some day or night a demon were to steal after you into your loneliest loneliness and say to you: "This life as you now live it and have lived it, you will have to live once more and innumerable times more and there will be nothing new in it, but every pain and every joy and every thought and sigh and everything un-utterably small or great in your life will have to return to you, all in the same succession and sequence." . . . Would you not throw yourself down and gnash your teeth and curse the demon who spoke thus? Or have you once experienced a tremendous moment when you would have answered him: "You are a god and never have I heard anything more divine." *

The idea seems to be that contemplating life's "eternal recurrence" will get you to seek—either in your past or in the future—a "tremendous moment" that would move you to praise as a god the being who informs you of this fate.

But I'm not sure why Nietzsche's proposal should work, why considering my life's eternal recurrence should move me to affirm any sort of life. One of my favorite movies is Juzo Itami's *Tampopo* (1985), a film about a search for an excellent ramen recipe. It's funny, original, experimental, and profound, with unforgettable characters and wonderful scenes of culinary indulgence and theatrical fun. I've seen it probably four times, and maybe I'll watch it a few more times in my life. Or maybe not. Even the best films aren't ones I necessarily want to watch over and over again. I've seen *Tampopo*. It's great. It's a favorite that I think about, talk about,

---

* Friedrich Nietzsche, *The Gay Science*, trans. Walter Kaufman (New York: Vintage, 1974), 273–274.

tell friends about. But I don't really care if I watch it again. And if I had to choose between another viewing of *Tampopo* and the nth *Fast and Furious* movie, I would absolutely choose the latter.

I think I feel the same way about my life. I don't think you could describe a life that I would want to live more than once. And my life is going alright so far. Maybe more than alright. There are so many moments when my life seems lovable, when a life-affirming electricity fills my limbs—a feeling that, sometimes, I want everything I do and am to absorb and express. Tremendous moments. Supposing things stay about as good as they are, I wouldn't want to live this life again. Once would be enough for me.

I'm not sure there's any description of a life whose *eternal* recurrence I would affirm or that I would affirm in a manner that embraces the spirit of *you only live once*. I'm sure that there are descriptions of lives that I would *not* want to live time and again. But why, if one of those were my life, should that make me want to affirm some alternative life or go in search of a heretofore unknown and tremendous moment? If I were to reflect on my life and find that it was the kind of life that I would absolutely not want to relive, then I might just feel depressed or hopeless.

Of course, *you only live once* might help here if it moved me to act in a way that, in turn, moved me to affirm my life or increased the chances that I would find my tremendous moment. But then Nietzsche's idea of eternal recurrence simply amplifies—to infinity—the fact that you have only one life to live, and so it magnifies, rather than answers, the question of why reflecting on this one life should give you reason to live one way rather than another, be any particular kind of person, or cultivate any particular sensibility or style.

It is certainly possible that I have missed something essential about Nietzsche's idea. He does seem to think that affirming life in the face of eternal recurrence is especially difficult and that only extraordinary individuals will succeed. Even so, consider more generally how odd it would be if the idea that you only live *once* could have the same inspirational effect as the idea that you live an *infinite number* of times. This suggests that numbers have nothing to do with it.

•

What is up with the "once" in *you only live once*, anyway? There is a very real sense in which I have lived more than once, and this does not diminish the existential imperative's power over me. My life has had different stages. When I was a teenaged skater, my values, desires, concerns, knowledge, skills, friendships—almost my entire life—were different from who I became in my late twenties and from who I am now, settling into my forties. And now that I am no longer young, no longer in my twenties or thirties, maybe there are different standards for embracing life that apply to me. The twenty-year-old options are different from those of someone at the bottom of forty. And I had a life-embracing youth, full of death-defying stunts, competing in the X Games, breaking bones, going big, and skating around the world.

But what should I do *now* to live up to the fact that you only live once? Drink a *third* pint of beer? Brazenly *not* drink the bottle of wine I opened and don't really like? Hike a smallish mountain? Spend an extra twenty minutes sweating all over the elliptical machine? The message is much clearer when spontaneity and adventure are easy. Maybe all

YOLO does now is whisper, *"Psst, why don't you plug in that bread machine?"*

At each stage of my life, it seems like the question is not whether I have one or infinite lives to live. The question is what I can do *now* to "live only once," to embrace life. It's about *living*—once, twice, as a twenty-year-old, as a thirty-year-old, as a new dad during a pandemic. If numbers have nothing to do with how *you only live once* works, then there must be something special about how *you only live once* gets you to think about life.

The Preservationist's objection reveals that there are two very different ways of thinking about life. The Preservationist's life is the life of your small, fluttering heart, your warm, bloody, delicate body. It is the life of rest, nourishment, protection, bodily comfort, and support. This life is precious, and because of that it is a demanding life, the demands of being part of this complex and volatile biological world. I hopefully sleep eight hours; I shower, feed myself, shave, poop, exercise, seek comfort, recover from illness and exhaustion, squirm to ease the pain in my back; visit doctors, dentists, and physical therapists. I work to pay for food, shelter, and insurance, and I hopefully find moments to space out and give my body and mind a break. Preservation accounts for most of my precious life.

Then there is this other life, layered on top and woven through, the life of passion and pursuit, of my dreams and aspirations, a life of love sought and realized, of beauty and community, of adventure and openness. It is a life I always want and don't always have, a vision I sometimes see with such clarity, a life animated in thought and action by the hope that *I shall flourish* along with my friends and family—that we shall hold each other up through our excellence, creativity, and goodwill, a life where *we flourish together*. Where humanity flourishes. The thought of this life fills my heart with love and hope, fills my lungs with breath.

Life is wild and precious and conflicted. Simply staying alive is demanding; the body's voice is loud and can overwhelm the call of the spirit. And the call of the spirit can send splinters through the body as your aspirations demand too much, your efforts overwhelm; you overwork, overindulge, overstress; are disappointed, disillusioned, abandoned; or realize slowly that your projects lack the meaning you thought they would have.

I think that when I am moved by *you only live once*, I don't hear it as *you have only one life*. I hear it as *remember: you are alive*. *You only live once* seems to work not by offering the reminder that death is certain or that life is precious, fleeting, full of meaning, or absurd. It offers the reminder that there is more to life than maintaining it, that you can reach for something beyond your body and little self—toward love, creative achievement, community, a higher beauty. Reflecting on the fact that you only live once helps you realize that you are not fully alive unless you are *actively valuing* this other life, being alive, reaching in this way. Jean-Jacques Rousseau, the Enlightenment philosopher (and proto-YOLOer), writes, "To live is not to breathe; it is to act; it is to make use of our organs, our senses, our faculties, of all the parts of ourselves which give us the sentiment of our existence. The man who has lived the most is not he who has counted the most years but he who has most felt life. Men have been buried at one hundred who died at their birth."*

---

* Jean-Jacques Rousseau, *Emile, or On Education*, trans. Alan Bloom (New York: Basic Books), 42.

Living is not just having a heartbeat. Rousseau suggests that being fully alive is a kind of *engagement*. It is engaging with life, living your life, in a way that keeps you attending, savoring, listening, examining, acting, and exploring in ways that inspire the "sentiment of your existence," that keep you attuned to and engaged with the value of being alive.

How can you live that way? How can you reliably engage with the value of being alive? The Preservationist surely gets something right: caring about the preservation of life *does* put us in touch with part of life's value. This caring is motivated by a profound sense of life's delicacy, its sublime fragility, its uniqueness and preciousness—all that can be lost in an instant. But these values are a small fraction of the full value of being alive. Being alive can be so many things. It can be thrilling, exciting, amazing, scary-fun, wild, weird, intense, profound, challenging. Attempts to avoid the openness, freedom, adventure, or even riskiness that keep us in touch with the full value of being alive tend to offend life by making it routine, subdued, fearful, predictable, closed-minded, or nonexperimental. To be moved by *you only live once* is to viscerally understand that your being alive, here and now, is so much more than having a heartbeat.

I think this is where *you only live once* draws its strength, from the fact that so much depends on the animation and reanimation of our sense of the full value of being alive. The structure of everyday life, of embodied, fragile, routine daily life, puts everyone in touch with the values that animate the Preservationist. You hardly have to do a thing. But the full and powerful voice of being alive—no one can hear that voice, or speak with that voice, without *doing* something, without being moved, bold, courageous, open, willing, engaged.

One reason I don't really care if I rewatch *Tampopo*, at least for the time being, is that I am still in touch with my sense of its value, its aesthetic value, its beauty as a film. I still like it and sense or feel its worth. If my vivid and complex sense of the film's value went away, then I would, as soon as I realized that, want to watch it again to revive my sense of what makes it so good. And doing so is as easy as rewatching the movie. Being alive is like this in a sense, but it is not quite as easy to stay in touch with, or to revive your sense of, its value. Being alive is a way of being whose value you must work to keep in touch with. Or, rather, it is a way of being that *just is* a practice of keeping in touch with its value. I want to say that that's what it is to be alive— it is to open yourself up to being the constant subject of this endless call. I want to know how I can keep in touch with the value of being alive—what practices I can take up to do so. I want to be able to tell you, in good faith, that it is possible, that there is a way of being alive that addresses The Question.

Maybe the Preservationist is on to something with their concern for the body. You naturally cling to life, and your body is the locus of it all, the ultimate source of everything you do. The Preservationist wants to preserve the body, but maybe you can be *devoted* to it. Maybe you can keep in touch with the value of being alive by engaging in practices of bodily love, as so many existential imperatives seem to promise: imperatives of wellness, self-love, treating yourself. And *you only live once* doesn't care how you respect its demands. Why can't you find a reliable and rich source of the "sentiment of your existence" in the fierce love of your delicate, precious body?

If you can, then the Preservationist does not need an answer. They need a recruit: you can learn to embrace life with the best metabolism, the healthiest gut microbiome, and the cleanest skin. To understand how to stay in touch with the value of being alive, you must study how your body's aesthetic is shaped by your mind's horizons.

Chapter 3

THIS BODY

I had an unforgettable sentiment of my existence once, when my teeth smashed through my lower left cheek. I'd slipped on some water while skating fast and ended up Supermanning ten feet through the air before slamming into the side of a skate ramp. I have a scar that goes through my face, on the inside and outside of my cheek, to remind me of this sentiment. There are better and worse "feelings of life" that you can seek and stoke. You might prefer the ones that respect your body and leave your face smooth, shiny, and blemish-free. Or at least intact.

But then again, you might not. It is probably no accident that YOLO is associated with bodily abuse. The rock climber broke a leg. The foodie has gout. The lead singer has polyps, and the harried writer has varicose veins. If your mind is inspired by the thought of your one and only life, then your body should be scared. The body is an abandoned temple. It is Play-Doh, the site of experimentation, augmentation, distortion, stretching, piercing, splitting, removing, enlarging—all in the name of this higher thing, this better, wilder, more beautiful thing. Septum, lip, nipple, and tongue piercings. Neck, face, lip tattoos. Ear gauging and tongue splitting, boob and butt implants. Fake tans, sharpened teeth, face-lifts and tummy tucks. People do not whisper mantras of wellness when they huck their bodies off a forty-foot cliff into the ocean.

To the Preservationist, treating the body well is an end in itself, a source of calm, confidence, love, and joy. Varicose veins, my god. Seriously, gout? Like *medieval* gout? Try the oatmeal with chia for once. Your body manipulations make you look like a lizard, but have you tried meditation? You live your life in, with, and through your body. You impinge upon and change the material world with your material self. Whatever you do, wherever you go, whoever you become—you do so in this fleshy way. And with your body you make more of life: you make your children, your works; you shape your life and your community. And so it is no surprise that the body is the focus of myriad existential imperatives that the Preservationist can wholeheartedly embrace. These are all imperatives to some version of self-love and bodily care, to wellness and bodily pleasure: the body is a temple, and preservation is its religion. Treat yourself, be well, love your body, embrace your beauty. Massage, steam, stretch, twist, cleanse, nourish, rest, and moisten your body into a blissful sentiment of your existence.

Yet it is so easy to feel the pull of each side. With one deep meditative inhalation, you treat yourself, and in your exhalation you whisper, "YOLO," and eat the whole muffin. (Or maybe you treat yourself with the whole muffin and find other ways to YOLO.) The body is a war zone. You fight on both sides, and this seems sharply irrational. One voice tells you to treat your body as a vessel of higher goods—of experiences, achievements, connections, transportations, fun, and thrills. If that means that you have to sharpen your teeth to look more like a lizard, then so be it. Another voice calls for an incompatible, risk-averse life of wellness. It seems that the war cannot be won. Maybe that is your plight—you are a contradiction, you contain multitudes or whatever.

But maybe there is a way for these voices to sing in harmony. Here, the Preservationists assert themselves in the register of the existential imperatives to self-love. The Preservationist claims that you can love life with no loss of spirit and existential sentiment while preserving your body *as long as you focus your love of life on the task.* Simply synthesize YOLO with bodily preservation. Say #fuckit YOLO and buy that $500 face cream.

Have you tried expensive face cream? *It's amazing.* World-class spas, all-day meditation and yoga, eating lightly, not drinking, relaxing, and getting a great night's sleep in high-thread-count sheets? Pure luxury. YOLO does not discriminate. If you have to drop your entire savings to spend a few weeks at a hot spring in Hakone with your face covered in mud, then where's my ticket to Japan?

•

Why does expensive face cream feel so good? Partly because, well, it just does. People put all kinds of things on their face. Some feel awful, some feel weird, some feel OK, and some feel amazing. Five-hundred-dollar face cream feels *the best*. But it also feels so good because it is $500. The price itself is part of it. It makes you feel special, precious. You put it on and you wonder, *Am I worth this $500 face cream?* And the face cream answers in the voice of your best friend, *Fuck yes you are.*

To feel precious is to feel lovable and loved. To love yourself fiercely (or expensively), then, is to boldly affirm your preciousness. When that fire dies, when others turn away, when you are no longer beloved, you might think you are no longer precious. In the opening passage of her beautiful reflections on love, bell hooks is quick to connect the feeling of being loved to the feeling of being regarded as precious: "To this day I cannot remember when that feeling of being loved left me. I just know that one day I was no longer precious. Those who had initially loved me well turned away. The absence of their recognition and regard pierced my heart and left me with a feeling of brokenheartedness so profound I was spellbound." *

---

* bell hooks, *All About Love: New Visions* (New York: William Morrow and Company, 2000), ix.

To recover and guarantee your preciousness, hooks suggests, you must salvage a "regard" you have for yourself and that you sense from others. You must see yourself in that way, and you want to see it confirmed in the eyes of others—to see yourself as beautiful in the beautiful look of another's gaze. I hope you can see this regard in your parents' gaze, and in the loving regard of your friends and family, but you must also find it for yourself.

Is the Preservationist right that you can find your preciousness in devotion to your healthy and vibrant body? A face cream might supply a fleeting moment of preciousness, but it won't *put you in your body*. But isn't that the goal? When you feel at home in your body *as y*our living, precious body, you radiate, you glow.

•

There is a reason to connect feelings of preciousness and being loved with your body. What makes the body unique as a medium of life is its perceivability. It is public. Your body is the locus of your *visible*, smellable, touchable, audible, tasteable life. To see yourself, you look at your body in the mirror;

to hear yourself, you vocalize; to present yourself in public, you wash, apply, dress, and adorn.

Because your body is public, you exist in a social world that sees you as embodied, and this social world attributes meanings to your body. The body can be perceived, so it can be discussed, and the social world has a lot to say about what makes a body *worth* perceiving—a whole system of norms: you aren't thin enough, tall enough, strong enough, smooth enough, well proportioned enough, light or dark enough. Your embodied life implicates you in embodied meanings, and almost everything you do with or for your body means something.

Bodies aren't perceived only in an instant. They are seen in movement, in how you walk, sit, look. They are heard in how you talk, in your word choice, your intonation, and the musicality of your voice. In much of social life, you *are* your movements, and movement is policed by complex systems of norms. Who can look at whom? Who can walk where? Can your voice be that loud or that quiet? Society attaches answers to these questions by attaching answers to bodies: Black, brown, white, male, female, rich, poor, large, small.

Does The Question even make sense when these social forces are so strong? The Question wonders about why anyone should value the one life they were unwittingly given. This is not far from wondering what you should do with your life, whether and how you should act. But doesn't society gives you the answer? If you are a man, you should dominate and control; if you are Black, you should act in this way and not that; if you are a woman, you mustn't, shouldn't, can't; if you are gay, straight, brown, white, rich, poor, educated, athletic, disabled—society has answers for everyone. Why isn't the answer to The Question simply a catalog of the social identity socially glued to your unchosen body?

The short answer is that society's answers to The Question are almost uniformly bad. Its answers do not give you your body—often it's the opposite: society steals, disfigures, disparages, and alienates you from your body, and in that way from yourself. Worse: social forces single out some bodies for especially bad treatment—female bodies, queer bodies, Black and brown bodies. These forces can maim, violate, and kill. In the face of these forces, bodily care—and "self-care" more generally, specifically as developed in the Black feminist tradition—is a powerful political strategy for maintaining and energizing political action and bolstering community.* But there is more to feeling at home in your body than keeping it healthy and sound, primed for the fight. To be at home in your body, your body must be your own: your figure, your voice, your bearing—to be at home in your body is to own or even define its movements through space. You have to find or make space to move. But the social forces regulating your movements are strong, and it is all too easy to internalize those forces and add your own voice to the chorus: *they are right*—I am too large, small, weak, strange, unworthy. I can't, wouldn't, shouldn't, mustn't, don't.

But social pressures around acceptable bodies can create social movements around bodily action. Pressure meets counterpressure, and new styles emerge, of dress, talk, dance, intonation, movement, and bodily confidence. Those movements, which are developments of bodily movement, are sourced in self-love.

---

* See Audre Lorde, *A Burst of Light: Essays* (Ithaca, NY: Firebrand Books, 1988), for a classic discussion.

•

Growing up, the backyard was my escape from the home defined by Dad's war. But I found a new backyard around the time that I asked The Question and sort of woke up. Three things changed then: we moved across town to join the aspiring middle class and try out homeownership, I got cheap rollerblades for Christmas, and a cement skate park opened a quarter mile from our new house. Within the year, the skate park would be my new backyard.

The skate park was home, my body rediscovered in spinning, flying, and flipping movement. So real and welcome was this newfound purpose that I was incapable of caring about the more acceptable things—girls, school, Boy Scouts, football—and it cemented the antipathy I felt toward my life in my parents' home.

The focus, intensity, and imaginative power that I honed in the backyard—every ounce went into skating and grew even more powerful. I was my body, and my body was fakie 720s, flat spins, switch-ups, sweat, scabs, contusions, muscle, and pubescent odor. I was speed, courage, injury, and invention. I was bacne, road rash, hip injuries, stitches, broken arms, and concussions. I was the essence of young, raw, shapable athletic power and blossoming skill.

I needed and sought nothing else, except friendship and guidance from the older skaters, whom I would follow everywhere, absorbing their skills and ways and incorporating them whole into my skating and into my life. What I found at the skate park became my life, which I found anew in the pools of cement poured in the middle of an apple orchard, in their sublime and subtle norms of respect, encouragement, danger, praise, pain, competition, and appreciation. And love. I found love there, in the passion I had for skating, in the support and admiration we had for each other, and in the ways I discovered I could move my body.

Within a few years, I was being featured in the skate magazines and videos. A year after that, I turned pro. I dropped out of high school to tour the world, compete in world-class competitions, film videos, shoot for magazines, and make money.

It was the late 1990s. I *was* the late '90s. I hung out with "Macho Man" Randy Savage (RIP), who autographed a Slim Jim for me (not easy to do; they are slim). I met Topanga from *Boy Meets World* on a video shoot and, like so many other boys my age, swooned. A budding romance? We hugged and talked on the phone for a while before losing touch. I adored Dave Matthews and frequently hung out with the band backstage after shows. I met Woody Harrelson there, and he seemed to be very stoned. We have the same birthday, which, he pointed out, we share with Haile Selassie. I did shots with Eminem while he barely entertained my dumb questions. I was in the X Games three times. I wore a hemp necklace, drank vodka Red Bulls and appletinis, and installed a minidisc player in my car. This little white boy knew every word of Natalie Merchant's album *Ophelia* and Nas's *It Was Written*.

My parents struggled to pay for the house they bought. The family van was repossessed, I think, or sold in desperation. I paid the mortgage once with the money I had earned from skating. So many of my memories of that time are red. My limbs are red from skating and falling. My shoulders and cheeks from sunburn and effort. My dad looks, smells, and seems red from some poison of insecure employment, Camel cigarettes, stress, anger, and pent-up love that would burst out unpredictably in a foul masculinity of demands, violence, and distance. That poison defined the home forever. The resentment and hatred I felt toward Dad, and, it seemed, he toward us, started melting everything else. In 2000, Mom and Dad divorced. I was nineteen.

Almost twenty years later, I started to understand how much that period of life affected me. My wife and I bought our house, our first, and I was gripped by what felt like a primordial shame that lasted months. I now owned my very own backyard and felt like I didn't deserve it. My instinct when I was nineteen, when my parents' divorce erased all remnants of family life, was to cling to the "backyard" that had seemed to be saving me. I doubled down on skating, and I was doing the best skating of my career. I was also taking more risks and paying the price in hospital bills, the abiding hint of death a reminder of the circumstances of my birth, circumstances that were themselves becoming history.

Home is not a house, and a house alone is not a home. Home is a place you make to your liking, a place you make your own. My strategy was, at its most fundamental level, to put my body in another place, away from the heat at the house. But my displaced body was not yet a healed body, a body at home in itself. The cliché is true: wherever you go, there you are. To really be elsewhere, my body had to be something else.

To find a home in my body, I made its movements my own. A new landscape is not a new life until you know how to move along its strange geometry and make it yours. I came to know every inch of the skate park, every bump and divot. Its graffiti became my art. I spent hours there, skating alone or with friends, from sunrise to sunset. I found ways to move, twist, spin, carve, grind. I styled my moving body almost beyond my own recognition, and well beyond that of my peers, in order to recognize it as mine.

I could not have found what I needed by merely taking care of my physical body. I had to move it, bend it, break it, and open it up to a new freedom. But even that was not enough—as influenced as I was by other skaters, I could not merely copy them. I had already done that. I was beyond that. I had to find my style in skating, and when I did, I became something else and skating, *my* skating, became my home. In becoming my body, my home, I created the love and preciousness I desperately needed. I created a source of self-love. The preciousness of my body was expressed in putting on skates and leaving the house, with all the physical harm that entailed.

But I pushed my body too hard, and time made its threats known to my limbs and joints. The home I found in 720s and flat spins didn't last. Time moves on, bodies change, and homes disappear.

•

Skating enabled me to inhabit my body anew, to find the rhythm of being alive in its new movements. But merely finding movement is not enough. Settling into a style is a matter of getting a *perspective* on the movements you find, a perspective that sees those movements in a certain light, approves of them, and ties them together, shaping a path forward through ways of creating new movements that fit and that adapt to new challenges. Finding a home for the body in movement is an effort in finding a perspective on your body and bringing that perspective to bear on your life.

This perspective is not merely descriptive; it is evaluative. A perspective is evaluative when it construes something as good or bad. Descriptive perspectives leave goodness and badness out of the picture. You can approach the world in both ways. You might see Zoe eating ravioli and describe her as slow, note that she is using a tiny fork, that there is sauce on her chin, chair, and shirt. You might *evaluate* Wolfe's eating ravioli as *awkwardly* slow, her fork as *inappropriately sized*, and the results as *wildly messy*. Or, if you learn the descriptive fact that Wolfe is a baby, you might evaluate his eating ravioli as *adorable*.

The perspective you need is evaluative—it is a perspective that is engaged with the goodness or badness of your body. But more specifically, it is a way of experiencing your body *aesthetically*: this movement, this stance, this activity feels right, fits; this one doesn't. One way of being in your body is powerful, elegant, bold, shocking, or wild. This other one is boring, extra, sketchy, or tame. One way to find a home in your body is to find your body's aesthetic. This is a creative and experimental effort involving the exploration of, and responsiveness to, different ways of being in your body, from ways of moving around, talking, and gesturing to ways of dressing, cutting your hair, or doing your makeup. This is also an ongoing effort, a negotiation between yourself, the people in your loving relationships, your other aesthetic pursuits, and your world.

It's not an easy perspective to find, and you have to contend with forces of masculinity and femininity that tell you what your style must be. And to echo every feminist ever, we are too easily swayed by nefarious sources of aesthetic bodily perspective. So you might, in the process, try to find your perspective by paying a lot of money for face cream. A $500 face cream, a luxury spa, even just a few solid days off, can offer hints of an aesthetic perspective on your body. They can seep into your imagination; you can let them overwhelm you, transport and transform you; and in doing so you bathe in more than mud. You bathe in the beauty you see in yourself when you are good at sinking into this perspective.

But these sources of perspective are often fleeting and cannot replace a bodily aesthetic that comes from a deeper source of creativity and action: your style. No one needs expensive face cream or luxury gyms to cultivate this perspective. The culture of wellness is culturally pernicious when it implies that you do. This aesthetic perspective is not something money can buy. Only time, experimentation, courage, aesthetic insight, and love can produce it.

In fact, this aesthetic perspective on your body is something you can cultivate even when your body breaks.

•

Late in his long and difficult life, when he was seventy-one years old, the revolutionary French painter Henri Matisse (1869–1954) was diagnosed with an abdominal obstruction (from a hernia he had suffered as a boy) and a potentially cancerous tumor in his colon. His doctors assumed he would die, but they held out hope for a radical surgery. The procedure worked and gave him thirteen more years of life. However, the last thirteen years of Matisse's life would be very unlike the previous seventy-one. After the surgery, his mobility was severely restricted, and he spent a lot of time in bed. He suffered from fevers, exhaustion, and the effects of various medications. He was still reeling from his recent separation from his wife, Amélie, who had left him in 1939 after forty-one years of marriage. And the physical difficulty of painting was matched by the doubts he had about the direction of his art, feeling that he had gone as far as he could with oil painting.* The disease spared him a semblance of his body and left everything else in his life an open question.

Some would prefer to die than to suddenly feel that they had lost their body, no longer belonged to it, were unable to move in the ways they had made their own over many decades. For Matisse, this loss was transformative: "My terrible operation has completely rejuvenated and made a philosopher of me. I had so completely prepared for my exit from life that it seems to me that I am in a second life."** In his second life, with a new self and a new body, Matisse transformed himself by transforming his work and turning to collage. With the help of assistants, he would apply paint to paper, then cut out and arrange the pieces into works that ranged from small to almost monumental, abstract to symbolic

---

* Hilary Spurling, *Matisse the Master: A Life of Henri Matisse: The Conquest of Colour: 1909–1954* (New York: Knopf, 2005), 428.

** Quoted in *Henri Matisse: Paper Cut-Outs*, exhibition catalog, St. Louis Art Museum (1977), 43.

or evocatively representational. Matisse called them "gouache découpés," or "gouache cutouts" (gouache being the type of paint). He regarded them as the culmination of his artistic life, spent producing groundbreaking work over fifty years. He thought they were the most self-expressive works he had ever made: "I have needed all that time to reach the stage where I can say what I want to say. . . . Only what I created after the illness constitutes my real self: free, liberated."*

What was Matisse freed from exactly? His feeling of liberation was no doubt partly release from the techniques and traditions he had spent five decades immersed in—those that defined his pre-surgery style, that he had helped invent, and that determined the course of twentieth-century painting all over Europe and the United States. Even the most revolutionary techniques can stagnate and solidify. Matisse seemed to see the new limitations of his body as an opportunity for renewal. With paint, scissors, and paper, he drew, carved, and constructed a new self.

―――――

*Quoted in *Henri Matisse: Paper Cut-Outs*.

But there is something puzzling about his thought that he was liberated. Some of the best works from this period were made after several years of perfecting his new technique, in the final period of his life. In 1946–1947, Matisse created two works, *Oceania, The Sky* and *Oceania, The Sea*. The large rectangular works are composed of various cut-out, plain, abstract figures in white against a uniformly beige background, evenly spaced and reminiscent of coral, seaweed, birds, and fish. Are these images of a place? Their titles suggest so, and in making them Matisse was inspired by his memories of a trip to Tahiti. He wrote,

This panel, [*Oceania, the Sea*] printed on linen—white for the motifs and beige for the background—forms together with a second panel [*Oceania, the Sky*], a wall tapestry composed during reveries which come fifteen years after a voyage to Oceania.

From the first, the enchantments of the sky there, the fish, and the coral in the lagoons, plunged me into the inaction of total ecstasy. The local tones of things hadn't changed, but their effect in the light of the Pacific gave me the same feeling as I had when I looked into a large golden chalice.

With my eyes wide open I absorbed everything as a sponge absorbs liquid. It is only now that these wonders have returned to me, with tenderness and clarity, and have permitted me, with protracted pleasure, to execute these two panels. *

Why does Matisse revisit these presurgery memories? It almost seems as if he is attempting to relive the life he lost, but what is liberating about that? What is liberating about embodying, in memory, paper, and paint, a self he can no longer be in a space he can no longer inhabit? From that perspective, these panels seem like mournful images of places and selves forever gone. So how has he discovered a new self? How is he liberated?

The mystery deepens when we learn about how a more youthful Matisse—nearly fifty years earlier, in his late twenties—discovered the aesthetic ideals that would shape his life and the lives of so many

---

* *Labyrinthe* 11, no. 3, December 1946, 22–23; reprinted in Jack D. Flam, *Matisse on Art* (London: Phaidon, 1973), 109–110.

artists. He grew up in the drab industrial north of France, in working-class Bohain, and didn't travel south to the Mediterranean until his honeymoon with Amélie in 1898. Matisse needed a clean break from the many challenges and setbacks he was enduring as a failing and ostracized painter in turn-of-the-century Paris. He and Amélie escaped to the island of Corsica, where Henri was blown away by the welcoming and friendly people and the intense quality of light and color on the island, its clarity a stark contrast to what he knew from his hazy northern homelands. This trip, like his surgery over half a century later, was transformative. One biographer writes, "He found himself jolted out of ways not only of seeing but also of thinking and feeling that had become second nature until now."* In their five months there, Henri produced fifty-five paintings.

Whatever Matisse felt about Tahiti was no doubt inflected by his formative experience in Corsica. What is striking about the images he produced fifty years later is that, despite being directly inspired by Tahiti and indirectly by Corsica, they

---

* Hilary Spurling, *The Unknown Matisse: A Life of Henri Matisse: The Early Years, 1869–1908* (New York: Knopf, 2005), 160.

seem to depict no place in particular. The decorative, geometrical figures create an *abstraction* of place imbued with Matisse's liberated style. Through these works, Matisse reactivated memories of leisure and indeed of *inaction*—a concept that defined his new way of being in his body. And he used these memories to evoke the current state of his body. But in these memories, it is *inaction* that is a source of "total ecstasy" and "protracted pleasure." Through his new body, with his new aesthetic, the inaction of total ecstasy becomes the total ecstasy of inaction.

Other works from this period similarly attempt to recreate spaces he could no longer physically inhabit and where immobility reigns alongside leisure, calm, and tranquility. *The Swimming Pool* (1952) is a large blue cutout of waves and splashes that lined the entire dining room of his apartment in Nice. *The Parakeet and the Mermaid* from 1952, among the largest cutouts he made, gave him a garden he could always visit. By that time, 1952, Matisse had mastered his new aesthetic and used it to create a world that defined his new self. Now Matisse could go to the garden, the swimming pool, Oceania, and when he did, he saw himself, a new and liberated self, staring back at him. He died in 1954.

As Matisse's death grew nearer, his images became more and more abstract. See, for example, the stunning nine-by-nine-foot abstract cutout *Memory of Oceania* from 1953. Matisse's increased abstraction meant increased access: the less concrete the place, the more easily it could float around—in his studio, his dining room—and the less it would remind him of the fact that the real places from his earlier life and self were lost to him forever. Matisse seemed to want to both relive a very specific memory of a very specific place and, through his work, strip that place of specificity so that he could be there again in his new skin. The more abstract it was, the more he could possess it. And in possessing the space he could inhabit, making it his own by making it his style, he created and found himself, newly embodied and in a new home.*

---

* I was initially inspired to think about Matisse's cutouts by the painter Eva Struble, whose work I wrote about for the San Diego art journal *Herein*. See "Nick Riggle on Eva Struble," *Herein*, ed. Elizabeth Rooklidge, January 17, 2021. Some of that text is reproduced here.

•

Matisse's transformation began in his unwell body but blossomed through his aesthetic activity, activity that, in turn, welcomed and affirmed his transformed body. As far as I know, he didn't say that his aged, disabled, dependent body was beautiful and precious, but couldn't he have? For it was love that produced his liberated style, love that he poured into his new aesthetic self—love for himself and his work, for the memory of his past and its transfiguration, for his being alive and transformed.

There is a lesson here about what it means to care for the body, to inhabit the body you have with acceptance and love, as precious, as a beautiful body. It is not a lesson you learn by repeating mantras of wellness. It is a lesson you learn when you practice a radical aesthetic openness to your body, to what it can do and produce, to what it can be in the light of your aesthetic perspective on it. The Preservationist gets part of this right by focusing their love of life on the loving preservation of the body. But in limiting bodily love to bodily protection, they miss out on the full value of being alive in your body. And so they miss out on wonderful sources of bodily preciousness, on ways of seeing yourself, and being seen, as beautiful.

And too often those mantras of wellness and bodily care come with their own aesthetic in the form of ideology, telling you how your body must look, how to be in the physical world—be aggressive, be strong, be fearsome and violent. But no body is born with an aesthetic imprinted upon it, and preciousness is not passive. Large, small, skinny, short, wide, top-heavy, bottom-big, fluent, awkward, sleek, spotty: the way your body speaks aesthetically depends on what you do with it. Whether the large seem meek or arresting, the small imposing or dear, the old youthful, the young savvy—it is all under the sway of aesthetics.

And through the aesthetic, you pour forth your beautiful works: your voice, composure, dress, tattoos, piercings, outfits, makeup, hairstyles, shoes, glasses, songs, dance moves, books, skate tricks, and gouache découpé. This is how you do things with this body to create sites of love that aesthetically communicate and fan out into the world, into, onto, and with other beautiful bodies, forming bonds that further amplify the world's beauty.

Sure, try a nice face cream or a few days in Corsica or Tahiti. But self-love is a home, not a resort. Whatever insights you have, whatever self-love you tap into, with $50 worth of cream absorbed into your shiny face—those must be incorporated into, and solidified in, ways of living that really engage you in being alive, that might show your life to be beautiful enough to be worthy of replication.

What are those ways, those actions, practices, and products? How can you engage in and create them? If you are going to treat and love yourself, find your style, surely there is no better time to do it than now. You needn't wait for your home to crumble, for your body to break. The only way to achieve it is through practice, and the only time to start is today.

Chapter 4

THIS DAY

I can't remember the details of what I did last Tuesday. I can tell you what I did last week, roughly. But which of those things I did on Tuesday or Wednesday, I don't know. If I thought about it long enough, I could probably come up with something, but if you're asking about any of the weeks before that, then it's hopeless unless it's recorded somewhere. You only live once, but you live your life in days or short stretches of days, which form a kind of spotlight illuminating little pieces of your months and years. If life is to be lived, then it is to be lived today.

Days are the homiest medium of life: not as grand as life itself and not as immediate, obscure, and venerated as this very moment. And so it is no surprise that days are the focus of some of the most famous and clichéd existential imperatives. Some single out this day—*no day like today!*—while others dis the future—*live like there is no tomorrow!* The most famous is, of course, the ancient *carpe diem*, often translated as *seize the day*.

A glance at the more common definitions of *carpe diem* reveals the same kinds of problems we have noted with the other existential imperatives. One definition implores you to make the most of the day, another that it tells you to enjoy life while you can. But these are very different, even incompatible thoughts. One seems to tell you to work hard, and the other seems to tell you to chill out. What does it mean to make "the most" of the day or to enjoy life, anyway? Chilling in a hammock, or in a place like Corsica, is nice and sometimes necessary, but it is not always better than using the day to help others, solve a hard math problem, practice philosophy, or teach the next generation of engaged citizens. Furthermore, people seem to use *carpe diem* as more than a friendly suggestion—it is a genuine existential imperative issued with apparent force as something everyone really should keep in mind. If *carpe diem* tells us to enjoy the day or get "the most" out of it, then we need to know what it means to do those things and why everyone should care about them.

A funny thing about *seize the day* is that, strictly speaking, days cannot be seized. I promise you've never grabbed one. Days are a certain length of time marked by the Earth's rotation around the sun. As such, like numbers and concepts, you cannot touch them; they exist in some other realm, unseizable. And everything we can seize—the clock, the calendar, the book, the plant, the coffee cup—is not a day. When someone says, "Carpe diem!" they are being, like Horace, the ancient Roman who made that phrase famous, a poet.

Poets deal in metaphors. And since a day can be seized only metaphorically, any insight will come from understanding the metaphor. As with any decent metaphor, there is a lot to unpack.

•

Let's be literal for a moment. When I seize something, my action is the expression of what I want and how I think, my desires and thoughts. I want the coffee, I aim for the carafe thinking that's where it is, and I take hold of it. I pour. I seize something to get what I want. What would it mean to act as if I could grab *a day* the way that I grab the coffee pot?

Grabbing is an action, and days are for doing. You wake with the sun and think about all the things you have to accomplish. In doing so you begin "taking hold of" the day (or not). One interpretation of *seize the day*, then, is this: *use the day to act on your desires.*

As opposed to what? You *have to* act on your desires. Your desires are simply the things that you want, and you can want things in different ways and to different degrees: you can *really* want some things, mildly prefer others. When you act against or without your desires—when you do things you want not to do—you are probably being forced to do them, or swayed by addiction or compulsion. And I hope that never happens to you. When you are really forced against your will, though, it is as if you didn't *do* anything: coercion, force, and addiction render your actions not fully your own. Even on your laziest, chillest, most uninspired and unconcerned day, you are acting on your desires, doing what you want. But presumably you still have something to learn from the ancient advice. *Carpe diem* is clearly telling you to do more than act on your desires.

In fact, it might even tell you to act *against* your desires. There are two ways I can make sense of actions that are indeed my own, neither coerced nor compelled, but where in some sense I am acting against my desires. One is what Aristotle called "incontinence." You are incontinent when you lack a certain kind of control over yourself. You cannot resist your desire to go to the party even though you are convinced you really need a good night's sleep, and now there you are, hanging and chatting until the early morning. But even here you *are* acting on your desires, even if they aren't the ones that you think you care about the most. The other sense in which you might not be acting on your desires is when you are acting openly, purely expressively, playfully, even wildly. Dancing with friends, being guided by the beat, absorbed in an erotic moment, or mesmerized by beauty. These are the times when you might seem to be flirting with new identities, exploring new values, discovering exciting new desires, or transforming or transfiguring the ones you already have.

Going to the party and dancing all night are surely things that *carpe diem*, or *carpe noctem*, can direct you to do. So if there is a sense in which you are not acting on your desires here, then *carpe diem* must not mean, simply, *act on your desires*.

Maybe the advice is not to act on your desires but to act on your best desires. When I seize the coffee pot, I don't pinch it or slap a floppy hand on it. I grab the handle, firmly, with anticipation and control. I really want it, so I act with conviction and clarity toward something I wholeheartedly want. Maybe *carpe diem* reminds you to act not on your half-hearted or everyday desires but on what you know to be good, worthy, self-defining desires. Your deepest and best desires. Call this the John Keating interpretation: in the film *Dead Poets Society*, the character John Keating, played by Robin Williams, tells his students, "Seize the day, boys. Make your lives *extraordinary*." I take it that drinking coffee and going to work are fairly ordinary. But if you realized your deepest and best desires, then wouldn't your life be remarkable?

Let's set aside two obvious problems with the John Keating interpretation of *carpe diem*. Wanting to be animated by your deepest desires is one of the more ordinary things you can do. Isn't that what you really want? Of course it is—you want to want the best for your life. So if you want to be *truly* extraordinary, *especially* remarkable, then do *absolutely nothing*. Sit on a chair and stare at a wall all day, every day, until you die. That would be notable. But that's obviously not what John Keating has in mind. Also, what's wrong with the truly ordinary? If life is such a gift, then why can't I live simply and simply enjoy this gift? It's as if you've been given a nice kitchen knife and told that merely having this knife commits you to becoming a Jacques Pépin–level chopper. Excuse me? Here's your knife back, and have a nice day. In this light the John Keating interpretation starts to look perverse: you have been thrown against your will into this mysterious and infinite universe—*now make your life extraordinary!*

But here's the real problem with the John Keating interpretation of *carpe diem*: do *you* know what your deepest and best desires are? I sort of do and sort of don't. I think I know some of them. I want what is best for my family; I want to write; I want to share whatever understanding I have achieved with others, with my students. But what *is* best for my family? Am I really doing the best for myself by writing so much? What understanding *have* I achieved? In fact, a decent part of my inner life seems to have been, and still to be, occupied with entertaining questions about my best desires. *What do I really want? Am I doing the right things? Are there changes I can make to do better by my family, friends, and myself?* I cannot begin to answer those questions without knowing something about who I am and what really is worth doing with the life I was unwittingly given. In other words, to follow this interpretation of *carpe diem* I would already need an answer to The Question, and so it cannot provide that answer.

I sometimes question the desires I hold dear, and when I'm in the grip of The Question I might think it is a little strange that I have any desires at all beyond needing to eat and use the bathroom now and again. Maybe the power of *carpe diem* is that it tells me to snap out of it. *Don't overthink it! Just go get what you want!* But even if I decide not to question *my having desires*, I still might question *the specific desires I have*. What if they are not the right ones for me, for now, for anyone? What if I am all twisted and stuck in my head with no clarity about what I really need?

Perhaps, instead, *carpe diem* tells you to pursue *the good things in life*. In this interpretation, to seize the day is to use the day to pursue *genuine* goods, to find real value in the world, to experience it, engage with it, create it. But no one can get *all* of the good things in life. What would that even mean? I cannot be all of the good kinds of people— I am just one person—and I cannot obtain all of the good things—I am a philosophy professor on a very modest salary with a family and a mortgage and a large cat. And even if I could afford to buy every cool thing in the world, what would I do with all of those things?

Carpe diem must be telling you to pursue *some* or even *a lot of* the good things in life. As I mentioned, people do connect the idea of *carpe diem* with *getting the most out of life*. Get the most out of life; squeeze the day for all it's worth. When I am almost out of mayonnaise, I seize my rubber spoon and scrape the sides of the jar until it's practically clean. I love mayonnaise. I bought that mayonnaise. I might even have made it. It is delicious. I love it and want it all. But I also have some stray bottles of beer in my fridge. Friends brought them over to this or that gathering, and they sit there for some reason. I live in San Diego. It is good beer. I might drink it. I might not. I don't really care to get the most out of the beer in my fridge.

Isn't life more like the beer in my fridge than the mayonnaise I bought? I didn't choose my life. I received it. I find myself here, alive, in my kitchen, staring at my beer and my dusty bread machine, wondering why I should get "the most" out of either. So what makes my life like my mayonnaise?

This is The Question in culinary form. (I know that this whole analogy really sinks or swims depending on how you feel about mayonnaise, but feel free to replace it with your favorite con-diment.) Why should I value something that was simply given to me, *even if it is valuable*? The prob-lem is exacerbated by the fact that, unlike the beer, it is not clear what makes life so good. For many of us, it is not at all obvious. And for too many of us, it is obvious that much of life is a sort of hell.

•

Isn't there something off about these ways of think-ing anyway—getting *the most* out of life, *seizing* the day, living to the *fullest*? They always seem to mean getting the most *for oneself*. They never seem to mean that you should think of others or work to soften, transfigure, or fix this broken world. Get the most out of *your* life, others be ignored or damned. These views reek of self-indulgence and construe the world as a child's playground. It is not a play-ground. It is something we are all building together, that we all have to oversee, maintain, and make good. In addition, if you lived literally every day to the fullest, or got what you think is "the most" out of life, then your standard of fullness would always increase, and you would have to continually seek more and more.

Grabbing, squeezing, exploiting, more, more, more. Aren't these suspiciously masculine, even aggressive metaphors? There is too much grab-bing in this world already. Grabbing money, tits, ass, necks, oil, land, nations—why should you live by metaphors of aggression, control, domination? Enough with seizing.

•

Surely *carpe diem*, along with all of the existential imperatives under consideration, shouldn't make you worse. Maybe the real impulse behind *carpe diem* is a little more mundane but even harder to achieve: to be a good person. Metaphorically or literally drinking all the beer and eating all the mayonnaise might be fun, but it won't (necessarily) make you a good person. And surely it helps to be reminded, every day, of the importance of being good—morally, ethically good.

Everyone can use a little moral inspiration, but existential imperatives seem not to be about morality, or at least not especially about the ethical life as such. The dictates of morality are like impartial rules that apply to everyone equally. In fact they might even be rules, laws issuing straight from the Good or from Reason Itself: be kind, don't murder, help when you can, don't lie, be considerate, respect other people. Everyone ought to recognize the value in these imperatives, but it is hard to see how moral dictates could capture the spirit of *carpe diem*. The rules would not have to dictate your day entirely— as long as you follow their constraints, the rest is up to you. But where the constraints of morality do speak, they tend to create uniformity—no one shall, everyone must, all cannot—and where they are silent, well, that's where we need them to speak up. You might be following the moral rules to saintly perfection without the slightest carpe in your diem.

I suppose I could try the next best thing and transfer or glue my life to something else, finding the rules of my life in the dictates of my devotion. I could give my life over to someone or something: the Cause, the Deities, the Moral Good, the Revolution—to Universal Love, or Whatever. But that would mean metaphorically giving away the one life I have and pinning all of my faith in the value of life to this other thing. Devoting my life to something other than living it would not necessarily be a waste, but whether it is would depend on the worth of the bigger thing. It would make an answer to The Question bigger than my little life, which would no longer be my own. There's only one of my life, and it is literally all and only mine to live. Giving it away might help me defer or ignore, but does not help me answer, The Question.

·

Where to turn, then? Horace offers a hint. The last line of his famous poem *Odes* 1.11 is this: *carpe diem, quam minimum credula postero*, often trans-lated as *seize the day, trusting as little as possible to the future*.

Trust as little as possible to the future: this line calls to mind another existential imperative, *Live like there's no tomorrow*. Of course, there *is* a tomorrow. It's tomorrow. While there is a small chance that you might not see it, there is a much greater chance that you will. In fact, the chance is so good, for the vast majority of people most days, that no one questions it without a special reason. And you do in fact depend on it quite a lot: if there really were no tomorrow, or if you knew that your life would end in a month or two, then why finish college, start a family, work on the novel, or open a new restaurant? Of course, you know that anything can happen at any time and that there is always a slight chance of death. So what could the impera-tive be telling you to do exactly?

Maybe it is to *pretend* or *make believe* that there is no tomorrow. When you pretend, you imagine or act *as if* something is the case while knowing that it is not. The stick is a gun! The grass is hot lava! The sidewalk crack is a vast ravine! To pretend that there is no tomorrow, then, would be to act as if death will, or very well could, steal you away at any moment, to make this thought more present or vivid. When you toy with the thought that you might die tomorrow, there is an impulse to think that you should live a certain way, with more intention, focus, and sincerity.

Death is the ultimate source of fear, the organizing principle of all horror. It scares everyone and everything. The most dejected hesitate before it, and the most serene prepare and plan for it. Why should the thought of your death inspire you to seize the day rather than curl up in anxiety or recoil in despair? It is reasonable to respond to impending death in so many ways: by soberly getting your affairs in order, by frantically finishing your creative projects, by spending all your time with loved ones, by indulging in every accessible pleasure, by sitting quietly and reflecting on the past, by falling apart. All of this is just life, so if *all* of these things are "seizing the day," then the imperative does not say much.

•

When I was eighteen years old, I was in Las Vegas at the end of a long skate tour that started in Vancouver, British Columbia, traveled all the way down the coasts of Washington, Oregon, and California, and came back up through Arizona and Nevada. Las Vegas was our last stop, and it happened to fall on the weekend of the tour photographer's thirtieth birthday. We were going out.

We were a big group, and we had probably six multiroom suites in a hotel just off the Strip. It was a Saturday night, and we all met in the rooms where the tour photographer was staying with the tour videographer. They had probably $30,000 worth of video and camera equipment with them, and since we were going out that night, there were also piles of other expensive substances.

I always toured with my guitar, so I brought it over to our preparty just for fun. I was out on a patio with some friends, fiddling with my guitar and smoking a joint, when I saw two large men in dark clothes and leather jackets walk into the suite. I didn't recognize them, and when I sized them up I noticed that one of them had a handgun. *Undercover cops*, I thought. Given the various substances lying around, I figured that our plans had just radically changed.

The men told me and my friends to come in from the patio, so we did. I brought my guitar in and set it against the wall. Then they told us to get down on the floor, facedown, hands out, palms down. I smelled the hotel room and wondered what was going on. One of the men instructed us to slowly take any valuables out of our pockets: our wallets, phones, stray cash. *Oh*, I realized, *we are being robbed.* As soon as I thought this, one of the men knelt on my back, and I felt the cold steel tip of a gun press into the back of my head. The man started counting down from 10: *Tell me where everything is, 9, 8, 7, where's everything hidden? 6, 5, 4 . . .*

My friends screamed and insisted that I did not know, that they already had everything valuable. The man let up and went in search of more goods. But minutes later he returned, cold gun pressing against my head again, and a more frantic countdown began.

Tell me where it is, he insisted, *10, 9, 8, 7, 6 . . .*

Fuck, I thought, *I am going to die on a hotel floor in Las Vegas . . . my life ends here on this hotel carpet in fucking Las Vegas. I fucking hate Las Vegas.*

Five, 4, 3 . . .

I was certain my life was over. I had no thoughts of heroic resistance or rescue. It was simply *This is the end, I guess. What a fucking shitty ending, smelling this idiotic carpet in this idiotic city.*

And then he was off me again, and within a minute or two they were out the door with all the media equipment and drugs. On reflection I realized that my guitar made me look like the resident of that suite. If I was playing a guitar there, then surely I was the one staying there, and if I was the one staying there, then I must know where everything was. The thing that brought me so much joy showed me the end of my life.

That was the only time so far in my life that I genuinely thought I was going to die, where I was *convinced* that I was witnessing my final moments. The real thought of my death was silencing. My life did not flash before my eyes; my heart did not flood with emotion. I just *did not want to die.* I was stoic in disbelief and empty resistance. My main thought, which I repeated silently, was simply *no no no no.* . . . It was the most purely negative experience I have ever had.

There is no telling how you will react to the real presence of your own death. Be yourself, then: death is pervasive—you live under its breath—while its imminence, for you, will always lie elsewhere, in other people, in distant times. Until it doesn't. And when death does impinge more directly on your affairs, visiting a friend, a family member, a neighbor or colleague, in a sharp stomachache that lasts for days, an odd growth, a bloody stool, it overwhelms you, affecting your entire being in unpredictable ways, your thoughts and emotions, your sleep, how you eat and think about yourself and relate to others. Death is too big to bring near to you undistorted in imagination. I hope you have a powerful and vibrant imagination, but here it will falter. Pretending that death is more imminent than it is might stoke an odd thought, but it's a fool's fakery.

•

Isn't it a little odd, anyway, to connect Horace's thought that you should trust as little as possible to the future with living like there is no tomorrow? You can depend on the future quite a lot while *ignoring* or *discounting* your knowledge of the coming days, so the thought needn't be about pretending that there is no tomorrow. Horace says to *trust as little as possible to the future*: you can trust *as little as possible* to the future while still trusting in the future a whole lot. You might eat as little as possible while still eating three meals a day.

I depend on the future in myriad ways. In fact, almost everything I do throughout my day—pay my bills, work on philosophy, cook, parent, water the plants, feed the cat—I do on the assumption that the future is forthcoming. What can you achieve by downplaying that fact?*

Right now I am writing outside, and it is three weeks into spring deep in Southern California, in San Diego, in the California coastal sage and chaparral ecoregion that extends across the border well into northern Baja, Mexico. You might think of beaches when you think of San Diego. There are beaches here, but that is not what makes San Diego fascinating. There are beaches all up and down this coastline, from Cabo to Kitsilano and beyond. San Diego's beauty lies more firmly in its canyons and coastal sagebrush, in the smell of sunbaked white

---

* For a stunning philosophical exploration of the assumption that the future is forthcoming, see Samuel Scheffler's *Death and the Afterlife* (Oxford, UK: Oxford University Press, 2013).

and black sage, in the searching and twisted cacti that thrive and glow in the searing desert light.

I am looking at this beauty now, in the form of a tall coral-like ocotillo that we planted in our backyard. It looks ancient and fearsome, its arms reaching and bending over six feet, fortified by hundreds of hard inch-long thorns. Its crimson flowers, always surprising when they appear in the spring, have just emerged, attracting hummingbirds and bees. As I write this, a hummingbird floats around it, hovering over the flowers and succulent leaves, the iridescent, fiery, dragon-like feathers around its neck shimmering as it inspects the ocotillo.

My current experience is unmodified by my understanding of my limited life. I am not thinking about death or that this is the last time I might see this. I am just seeing it, observing the ocotillo with calm and care. Maybe I will die tomorrow; I am not thinking about that. The ocotillo does remind me of time—it looks ancient, reminds me of tenacity, survival, even pain or death in its hostile, defensive spikes. Those thoughts are associations evoked by the plant and may inflect my experience of its beauty, its aesthetic value.

When I am engaged by this beauty, my future is a misty horizon, vaguely present but out of mind, like the sound of construction in the distance. I haven't lost myself; in fact I feel more like myself, more open, more attentive, mellow with a hint of love for the beauty. The misty horizon could darken, thicken into a fog; I could easily fall prey to thoughts about money, deadlines, family. Or, it occurs to me now, I could dwell on the fact that there are weeds poking out of the rocks near the ocotillo, Bermuda grass, the worst. I should pluck it. Did I pay the bill? The ocotillo's beauty silences these thoughts.

I could change my experience by pairing it with the thought of an empty future. I might imagine that I will die tomorrow, or disappear, or that this is the last time I will ever experience this beauty. Does this decrease my trust in the future? Perhaps, but I prefer the other experience, when thoughts of life or death were absent and the experience was not framed by time in one way or another. There is a big difference between loving something while implicitly trusting that you will live longer and doing so explicitly thinking you could die at any moment.

I could have been unaware of this beauty, especially if I was anxious about the weeds or fixated on the future, on what I had to get done *today, today, the only day*. But doesn't *seize the day* encourage such a fixation, telling us to do more, get more, be more? *See the beauty, pay the bill, do the chores, run the miles, harder faster more productive.*

Not if you listen to Horace. Horace tells you that *carpe diem* is about *trust*. When I lessen my trust in the future, I can put it elsewhere, in the present. But what am I trusting the present to do? What am I trusting it for? When I trust in the future, I trust it for its value, for the goods I hope it will bring if fortune favors me and my efforts succeed— the finished book, the healthy baby, the spare cash, or the future itself, the furtherance of my life and, hopefully, the flourishing of my being alive.

If I were to trust as little as possible in the future, then I would have to discount the good I hope it will bring. I would have to look elsewhere for value: for the things I might desire to make my life worth living. I might still vaguely trust that the future will be good, if only by *being my future*, but in trusting as little as possible in the future, I commit to ignoring that fact and so look elsewhere for the value I need to drive and define my life.

So maybe Horace's point is really about *focusing on value*. Advice about focus is especially apt when you are inclined not to. And if you are like me, then you are no monk, and your future looms large in and often crowds out your present, often to good, if outsized, effect. But if I stop fixating and depending on the future's goods, a whole other world opens up, the one where I currently am today, this day, a world full of amazing and beautiful things, like this blooming ocotillo.

And the smell of the early-spring air, the rhythmic and subtle sway of the passionfruit vines in the slightly cool and light wind, the music playing in my earbuds as I write about beauty, the subtle pulses of inspiration that thrive on and feed my writing, thankfully, and now the radiant warmth of the desert sun as it bounces off the decomposed granite, the calm of my regular heartbeat, and, when I focus on it, this feeling of gratitude that—why?—soars up through my spine if I let it. The glowing ocotillo that foregrounds a peach tree in full bloom, heavy with light pink petals, carmine buds, and, if I squint, yellow-tipped pistils. The look of concentration on my wife's face right now as she works (so diligently, so well) across from me. The softness and beauty of our cat, who wandered out to check on us, whose fur sways in the wind, and who almost died a couple of months ago and is now dying slowly from kidney disease.

My attention to these things puts my "dependence on the future" out of my mind but not out of existence—and it transforms my inclinations to act. I reach out and touch my cat; I smile at my wife, who smiles back; I get excited about all the peaches we will eat soon; and I want to write. The goods I notice now seem almost to reach out from my noticing them into some better future and back again into this beautiful present. And in doing so they reach inside and transform my sense of self. This reorientation to present value changes how I seem to myself because my awareness of value is intimately connected to my will, my ability and inclination to act. *Carpe diem* might not tell me to act on my desires, but I think it tells me to act on *these* desires, the ones that arise when I open my will to this beauty.

When I am more open and attuned to the world's present value, I feel more at home in the world I am in: who would I become if I let this world in more often, if I made it more of my regular home? When my sense of self "depends on the future," on the goods I expect time to deliver, the current world is never enough, and so my self is always incomplete, lacking, the present world a stepping-stone made of sand that disintegrates when I step away from it onto the next one. Shifting my attention, love, and will toward this day returns the world to my self and puts me in a place to return my self to the world.

.

Are we seeing the glimmer of an answer to The Question? Maybe, but I don't yet know why. Why do I feel this way when I lessen my valuing trust in the future and notice and dwell on the ocotillo, the writing, the sky? Why do *these things* provide for me and for you in this way; why do they have this value? So far I have not an answer but an echo, and I can say this: the way you think about your life when you think you have only one echoes the way your sense of life expands and opens when you "trust as little as possible in the future." The practice of being alive is present in both.

What does any of this have to do with "seizing the day"? There is a tension between seizing something and engaging with the value that is presently before you. To seize is to obtain, and to obtain is to intend, act, succeed—it is to move yourself into the future to get what you want. So seizing requires a focus on the future that is connected to the present—it requires seeing the present as future. It is no wonder, then, that people associate *carpe diem* with getting *the most* out of life, with working harder, longer, better. Reaching your hand into and seizing the future by seeing the future's promise in this day. But lowering your trust in the future's value and engaging with the value presently before you needn't have anything to do with "seizing." It is more a matter of *shifting, opening, caring*. It's attending, noticing, tuning your will and attention away from the future and anchoring it, and yourself, in this day. Rather than imposing your will on the world, you let the world you see through your aesthetic eyes shape your will. This has nothing to do with seizing.

•

Let's return to it, then. The Latin word *diem* is straightforward, but what about *carpe*? What does that mean? *Carpe* is the second-person singular present active imperative of the word *carpō*. If you were translating the English word "seize" into Latin, you would not look to the word *carpō*. *Rapio* and *capio* would be more suitable. *Carpe* means to *pluck* or *harvest.** Horace's advice is not to seize but to *pluck* or *harvest the day, trusting as little as possible to the future.* To harvest something, you have to know what is harvestable now—look at the apple; it is ripe and delicious, the corn sweet, the river water pure. If you wait until tomorrow or the next day, the fruit might spoil, the crows might get the corn, the water might freeze. The metaphor of harvesting the day invites you to take a very different approach to this day: *see the day as you might see a lush field.* The day is a field of flowers, unfurling here and there.

---

* Maria S. Marsilio, "Two Notes on Horace Odes 1, 2," *Quaderni Urbinati di Cultura Classica*, New Series, 96, no. 3 (2010), 117–123.

I imagine the American poet Mary Oliver knew this. Her poem "The Summer Day" can be read as a riff on Horace's *Odes* 11.1:

Who made the world?

Who made the swan, and the black bear?

Who made the grasshopper?

This grasshopper, I mean—

the one who has flung herself out of the grass,

the one who is eating sugar out of my hand,

who is moving her jaws back and forth instead of up and down—

who is gazing around with her enormous and complicated eyes.

Now she lifts her pale forearms and thoroughly washes her face.

Now she snaps her wings open, and floats away.

I don't know exactly what a prayer is.

I do know how to pay attention, how to fall down

into the grass, how to kneel down in the grass,

how to be idle and blessed, how to stroll through the fields, which is what I have been doing all day.

Tell me, what else should I have done?

Doesn't everything die at last, and too soon?

Tell me, what is it you plan to do

with your one wild and precious life?*

If Oliver were "seizing the day," then she would not be strolling so idly. No, she falls down. She stares at this grasshopper. Her actions are not organized in favor of some concrete or well-imagined future good. Her actions are not even an expression of her deepest and best desires, at least not ones she has clearly articulated to herself. No, the world *itself* is her guide as she engages with it through her attentive eyes: the chance encounter with a fascinating grasshopper, wandering through the field all day. Falling down in the lush grass is fun; grasshoppers are wonderfully strange. Oliver is *literally in a field*, harvesting its goods. The poet is the grasshopper falling down in the grass, at home in the grass, her eyes also "enormous and complicated."

---

* Mary Oliver, "The Summer Day," reprinted in *Devotions* (New York: Penguin Press, 2017), 316.

She knows how to pay attention to the day, to the field of grass, plucking away, finding poetry in it.

What else should I have done, she asks, follow my "plans" for the day? And with a dose of sarcasm, she asks what do you "plan" to do with your one wild and precious life? Should you make a list: arrange to visit the field, desperately look for grasshoppers, carefully count of those you have found, and fall down in the grass at least once? Or should you open those wild and complicated eyes and venture forth?

When you understand *carpe diem* as *get the most out of life, get shit done, grab–tackle–seize the day*, then although it is questionable advice, at least you understand exactly what it is telling you to do. In that sense it is down-to-earth, and that is good because *carpe diem* is supposed to tell you how to live. But when you understand it as *harvest the day*, it might seem to lose some of its force. After all, who among us can be in a (perhaps metaphorical) field all day, skipping and falling down, staring at bugs and writing poetry? Where does that fit into this life of work, bills, kids, exercise, friends? What if the only field you know about is a vacant lot in the middle of the city? And even if you do have some field time, surely you cannot visit every day. What should you do in the meantime?

The answer lies in the fact that these days are not some field you happen upon, waiting to be harvested by your complicated eyes. They are also something you create. The problem with the metaphor of plucking and harvesting when applied to a lush field is that it suggests that everything good is already there to be plucked, harvested, and exploited for your pleasure, and Oliver's poem might seem to reinforce this thought.

But it is important to notice that Oliver did not merely enjoy falling down and sitting in the lush grass or staring at the weird bug. *She made poetry. She drew you to the field.* She transformed the field with play, made poetry out of it, and offered it up to you. You and I: we read her poetry, and there we are. In the field, part of it, with her.

And this makes the "diem" so much more than a tool that serves the self. It harbors the present good, which has the power to transform that self— the diem is always a new day. When you trust as little as possible in the future, you are more open to the value in the present. And this openness is not purely passive or receptive. It is active and creative, transforming how you act toward and think about yourself and others. The beauty you find with your complicated eyes calls you to it and renews itself through you in how you engage with it, with your special attention and care, with motivation that issues in creativity, play, or poetry. And you sling this beauty back into the world's present value for others to find.

And of this process, the engagement with and reproduction of beauty, I want to say: it lies at the heart of being alive. I want to say that because it seems as if continued, skillful, creative engagement with beauty always produces answers to The Question. But how can I say that to you? How can I show you that if you pay attention, if you open your complicated eyes and live your life with the knowledge that it is precious and wild, then you will find these answers and offer them up? Here, as elsewhere, time is a great teacher.

Chapter 5

THIS TIME

You live in and with time, and it is an awkward companion. In the form of the past, it can be a haunting shadow, an embarrassment, an unwelcome reminder. In the form of the future, a prankster, an ominous horizon, an unreliable coworker, uncertainty itself. And the present moment, the exalted now, is so elusive that entire religions worship it and self-help gurus peddle it. Time apparently *passes by*, but what does that even mean if it's always *now, now, now*? Time is omnipresent and envelops us all. Everyone has to make good by it. So much of your life is and will be spent striving for a home in time.

Who has found one? Who has made peace with their past, their era, their place in history, their orientation to the future?

It is natural to seek understanding and guidance in your family origin stories, stories of past bodies piled up in splinters of time, those vague and always embellished sources of value and identity that further bind a family and fleck the days with pride, hope, solace, shame. Your ancestors, your past, your bringing them into your future with you, establishing yourself in their lineage. You treat your origins as a home in time, extending yourself back into the past in a way that, you hope, will anchor you and your ancestors—in the present.

My dad served two tours in the Vietnam War. He was nineteen years old when he set foot in Saigon in 1967, and he left several years later with a Purple Heart medal and his whole life ahead of him. As a helicopter door gunman and mechanic, his life expectancy was a matter of days (nearly twelve thousand helicopters were shot down or crashed during the war). It is astonishing that he's alive. And so it is remarkable that I am alive, I, this descendant of that lucky or unlucky man whose life should have been obliterated in the hellfire of perverse ideology and stupid power and who, since it wasn't, was made never to forget that fact.

Looking further back, my blood seeps into the very beginnings of US settler colonialism. My middle name is "Alden." As my family tells it, we are several of the many descendants of John Alden Sr. (1598–1687), the storied crew member of the Pilgrim ship *Mayflower*, who, when he arrived on the East Coast of what is now the United States, decided not to sail home and settled in Plymouth instead. He and Priscilla Mullins (1602–1685) had ten children and were great-great-grandparents of the second president of the United States, John Adams.

Whose origin story is a clear and true story of home and hope, anchoring their life in time past and projecting it like a rainbow into the future? Among my ancestors are a confused and place-less people who escaped their homeland to build their new home on top of the homes of so many others, guided all the while by some divine delusion, a sense of superiority they saw gleaming off their white skin and strange religion and lighting up a land they mistakenly saw as primitive and needful. I come from them; I inherit their ways.

Ways that led my father to war and trauma, which I also inherited. The tides of history washed my ancestors to the shores of the Pacific Ocean, to California, where I was born and now live. I love this beautiful state, but how much of my love can be grounded in its history, in the genocide—the torture, enslavement, displacement, rape, kidnapping, murder, and indoctrination—of countless indigenous Californians?

So much history is selective mystification, chosen to support either the present, with its habits, values, and institutions, or some hopeful vision of the future—as if reaching back farther in time to find a good story can make time itself better, more intelligible, maybe even more favorable. Such sleight of hand has its uses, but it has no hope of answering The Question. And much of human history, so far, is a dark and terrible story where love lurks only in the long shadows of war, oppression, murder, pain, inequality, and injustice. I want a home on Earth, but how can I find a home in time past?

•

When I was twenty, I thought I found an answer to The Question. I had the most mysterious experience of my life, one that I still do not understand. I tried for years to understand it and gave up. Now it just sits in my past as a mystery, and as I age, my connection to it loosens and grows stranger. The experience was so remarkable because time itself seemed to stop, or, rather, to stop existing altogether.

I was in my car waiting at a long and boring stoplight in the middle of the afternoon. I looked out beyond the townscape to the horizon. In the distance, a series of low, sunbaked, grassy hills sat beneath an everyday blue sky. When I looked above the hills at the sky, it seemed to me, all of a sudden, that there was no real difference between me and everything else. This wasn't confusion; it was a conviction, as if I were finally realizing the deepest possible truth. It seemed like the *only* truth. *This is reality*, it seemed to say. My sense of self dissolved, time seemed to disappear, and I seemed to be one with something eternal. There was a distinct sense of timelessness or infinity that I struggle to describe, and along with it a profound clarity about death—death, I realized in that moment, was nothing, could not be anything, since I am timelessly one with the infinite universe. This might seem like a terrifying experience, some strange hallucination or otherworldly possession. But it wasn't. The moment it started and as long as it lasted—indeed, the very first thing I noticed when it started—my body was flush with love in beholding a most profound experience of beauty. I remember the feeling of love more than anything, and some remnant of it still lights up my heart as I recall it, as I write this.

As I was driving away and pulling onto a highway I had driven down a thousand times, my only thought, my only recourse in that moment, was the Christian religion my mom practiced but that had always alienated me: "Oh," I said out loud in the car as I pulled onto Highway 12, "my god." The following days I felt physically light, emotionally buoyant, and joyous with what remained of that pure love that seemed to light up my blood.

What the fuck was that? This question, in that form, has not left me since then. Did I glimpse some pure reality? Did it have something to do with the psychedelic mushrooms I had eaten with my friends a few times? Did I somehow make up this memory and convince myself that it was a real experience? No, it really did happen. I tried to understand it by studying philosophy and the world's religions—a serious effort since I was a scrappy high school dropout who, until then, had cared only about ripping through cement bowls, doing backflips and 720s, and grinding rails. For years afterward, I tried to recreate the experience through Buddhist meditation. I failed (though I did get damn good at meditating). Since then, I have simply lived with the thought that maybe time—and love and death and selfhood and beauty and existence itself—is not nearly what it seems.

None of this makes The Question easier to answer. Not only did the universe bend and fold itself into my tenuous, uncalled-for existence, but now it tells me that nothing comes into or leaves it. My very sense of having come into existence, of being in time, of death, is some illusion it saddled me with. Now it's just fucking with me.

•

One glaring feature of the experience was *the present moment*, which I was utterly absorbed in. My mind seemed to merge with or transform itself into the present, silencing all thoughts of past and future, of origin and destiny, by erasing my normal sense of time passing.

Some say that this is where you should focus as much of your attention as possible: in the now, the present moment, the supposedly only really real time. The reasons offered for living this way are as numerous and confusing as the imperatives that advocate it. The English writer and scholar of Buddhism Alan Watts promotes the idea: "For if we open our eyes and see clearly, it becomes obvious that there is no other time than this instant, and that the past and the future are abstractions without any concrete reality. Until this has become clear, it seems that our life is all past and future, and that the present is nothing more than the infinitesimal hairline which divides them. . . . It is rather the past and the future which are the fleeting illusions, and the present which is eternally real."*

Say what? The past and the future are illusions, but they are real and they exist, but only the present exists? OK, let's give Watts this oddly phrased idea: the past and the future are illusions that exist in the present as *real* illusions. Why would it follow that you should pay no attention to them? It might

---

* Alan Watts, *The Way of Zen* (New York: Vintage Books, 1957), 199.

be therapeutic to remind yourself not to take the illusions of past and future too seriously, but illusions are fucking cool. Especially when you know they are illusions. And the past and the future *seem so real.* If they are illusions, then they are really powerful ones, as epic as the best magic tricks or the giant rising moon on the horizon. I'm going to pay attention to them. Of course, you shouldn't get too caught up in illusions, but you definitely want to experience the cool ones, talk about them with friends, maybe take a picture.

The Russian writer and Christian anarchist Leo Tolstoy expresses a similar thought through the "hermit" character in his short story "Three Questions": "Remember then, there is only one time that is important—Now! It is the most important time because it is the only time when we have any power."* Tolstoy does not deny the existence of past and future; he denies their value. Only one time is important: the present. Why? Because it is the only

---

* Leo Tolstoy, "Three Questions," in *Walk in the Light and Twenty-Three Tales*, trans. Louise Maude and Aylmer Maude (New York: Orbis Books, 2003), 351.

time when you "have power"; it is the only time you can do or change anything.

Tolstoy's hermit seems to think that all action takes place in the present moment. But it doesn't. Myriad dead writers, politicians, rebels, and inventors did things during their lifetimes that are still influencing the present. And even if you are living in the present, why not work for a better future? I want to say with conviction that *the future is important*, that it matters for our lives and for the lives you launch into it. The present is not the only time that matters.

The American naturalist and transcendentalist Henry David Thoreau also thinks that you should *live in the now*, but his attempt to deliver this idea produces a confused and useless mass of existential imperatives: "You must live in the present, launch yourself on every wave, find your eternity in each moment. Fools stand on their island opportunities and look toward another land. There is no other land, there is no other life but this."*

---

* Henry David Thoreau, *Journals*, entry of April 24, 1859, https://hdt.typepad.com/henrys_blog/2010/04/april-24-1859.html.

You have to live in the present and make the most of life because the future is nothing and you only live once! So often the attempt to make sense of the power of existential imperatives results in repetition and circular nonsense:

> Seize the day because you only live once!
>
> You only live once, so live in the moment and make the most of life!
>
> The moment is fleeting, so live like there's no tomorrow and seize the day!
>
> Live in the now and YOLO it up because you might die tomorrow!
>
> You only live once, so treat yourself and squeeze every moment for all it's worth!

•

The American philosopher John Martin Fischer takes a different approach. He thinks that we should pay special attention to the present moment, but not because it is supposedly the only time there is.*

---

* John Martin Fischer, "The Problem of Now," *Aeon*, January 8, 2021, https://aeon.co/essays/the-metaphysical-claims-behind-the -injunction-to-be-in-the-now.

Suppose that the present moment is indeed the only time there is. It follows that the future and the past do not exist. Does that mean you should focus only on the present? No. Fischer points out that you can attend to any number of things that do not exist. You can think about the good and bad qualities of Virginia Woolf's fictional character Mrs. Dalloway, about what she will do after the party, whether her life will change much, or whether she should or shouldn't do this or that. Even if the future does not exist, you can still think about your fictional self in the future. In fact, I would say that doing so would be an excellent idea. The mere fact that only the present exists does not imply that you should focus only on it.

There would need to be some further argument to establish that you should not focus on a fictional past or future. But what argument could be given? It's a genuinely good idea to plan for your future and to make good with your past, even if this involves thinking about fictional things. The past lingers and haunts while the future looms. You cannot ignore them. You might also think about your unlived life. Or unlived lives. Not lives you did or might still lead but lives you *might have* lived, or lives you *could* but probably won't lead. Maybe these are all thoughts about fictional or otherwise unreal selves and lives. So what? All the better for our poetic, literary, fantastical, philosophical minds.

The thought that you should *live in the now, attend to the moment, be here now* is not supported by this moment's purported singularity, its importance for action, or the illusoriness of other times. Is there another way to understand it?

Well, maybe, if you're monkish enough about it, focusing on the present will give you an experience of deathlessness, timelessness, infinity, love, and profound beauty. But having had such an experience, I find it as mysterious and vexing as wonderful. And although the experience involves an indescribable sense of absolute selflessness, it doesn't make you disappear. You still have to live the life you didn't ask to live. Despite the exhortations of so many religions and self-help gurus, living a good life does not require that you experience some Beyond.

There are other reasons to attend to the present moment. First of all, it is a useful skill that takes practice. You know this well if you've ever tried to meditate or even focus on anything for any length of time. Once practiced, attending to the now, the unfolding, mellow passing of time, can reduce stress and anxiety. Most people could use that skill. But notice that this does not produce a *categorical* or even very general reason to attend to the moment. It produces a hypothetical or conditional reason: if you're stressed or anxious, then breathe, slow down, attend to the passing of time, the rising and falling of your breath. But if you're not stressed or anxious, well, carry on.

Fischer himself adopts a different reason to attend to the moment. Often your attention is wholly absorbed in everyday events and tasks: making breakfast, getting to appointments, attending the meeting, cleaning the kitchen, watching the TV show. When it is, you lose yourself in the experience and have trouble separating your feelings from your sense of self: you identify with your anger when there is traffic on the way to work, with your frustration at yet another sinkful of dirty dishes, with your boredom at the meeting. But when your attention is not so absorbed in experience and activity, it tends to flit from one topic to another: did I pay the electric bill? Yes, yes, I did. But I think I still have to pay the water bill. I guess

I'll do that tomorrow. What's the plan for tomorrow? Gotta check my calendar. I think I'm free in the evening. I'll have to shop for groceries after work, though. Work sure has been stressful. So glad I planned a little getaway in a few weeks. I'm going to get a new swimsuit. Maybe that's what I'll do on Saturday. I wonder if Chelsea would want to come. Meh, she usually works on Saturdays. Whoa, wait. Hey, the kitchen is clean!

Is there a better way of paying attention, being in the moment? Fischer recommends cultivating a kind of *clear-mindedness*, a quality of attention that he calls *being* here now as opposed to being here *now*. You can actively attend to your surroundings in the moment without getting so caught up in the moment that you fully identify with your thoughts and emotions. When you practice *being* here now, you become the watcher of your experiences and emotions. You are able to separate your thoughts and feelings from the one who is aware of those thoughts and feelings and see them, along with everything else that is happening, as manifestations of an ever-unfolding reality. You can witness, with awareness and clarity, this unfolding. You can then observe it without getting too caught up in it, and this gives you greater freedom and control.

Fischer does not think that losing yourself or being absorbed in your activities or experiences is always bad. Rather, he thinks that another way of attending to the moment is also good, and at times extremely important. But is it good in such a way that you should try to live your life like that, so good that it gives the existential imperative—*attend to the moment, live in the now*—the kind of meaning and force you should expect from existential imperatives?

There are clear benefits to cultivating the kind of attention Fischer recommends. Once I had a stomachache for approximately eighteen months, a sharp and shifting pain in the middle of my gut that was accompanied by a zombie horde of gastrointestinal symptoms. An endoscopy revealed nothing, and no one—not a highly educated crew of specialists, generalists, naturopaths, and friends—could figure out its cause or fix it. So I lived with the pain. But I noticed that whenever I *identified* with the pain, I suffered even more. *Why me? Why can't anyone fix this? Is this merely unpleasant or like* really *bad?* Those aren't unreasonable thoughts, but I was strongly tempted to attach them to my felt pain, and when I did, the pain worsened. I suffered beyond the pain. If I wasn't careful, then every time the pain's intensity increased, those thoughts returned as if they were just another symptom attached to the pain. Only when I separated myself from the pain and modified my awareness of it in the way that Fischer describes was I able to let those thoughts go and live with the pain, or *along with* the pain. By not letting the pain dominate my life, I could carry on.

That is a good thing. But what if you don't have chronic pain? Most of my feelings and emotions—even much of my sadness, anger, frustration, and despair—*I want to feel*. Fully, immediately. They are me. I don't want to watch, avoid, or ignore them. I want to be them. Understood in this way, living in the moment might be good advice for some people, but an existential imperative designed to keep you an attentive witness of life's passing has no hope of answering The Question.

•

These ways of understanding the idea that you should live in the moment are all *disengaging* in a sense. They are ways of disarming the past or future, or of pushing against the pull that distraction, pain, and difficult emotions can have on you. Disengaging from what you feel or think can help you regain control over a life that may have spread too wide and slackened over a gulf of pain and suffering. But at best these are ways of regaining a life you might have lost, not necessarily of amplifying the life you have.

When you do cultivate the skill of actively attending to the present moment, you aren't stuck seeing things merely as they are; you don't have to be a mere watcher of the basic world. Your eyes can be big, wide open, and at the same time *complicated*. You can complicate them. When you are free to watch, you are free to watch for the aesthetic character of things, their elegance, boldness, sleekness, grace; their fascinating aromas, auras, textures, feels, sounds. You can let your feelings and emotions resonate in response to the objects of your active aesthetic attention, like the musical notes of struck chords, where almost anything you can engage with is a potential instrument. And when you are good at getting into or being open to this state, certain things can strike you, can emerge and resound as salient: the way the trees sway in the wind, the sound of birds chirping in the distance, the smell of jasmine flowers baking in the sun, the way a person gets out of their car, the rain splashing on the street in front of your house.

When I engage with the aesthetic present and feel drawn to what I find there, I *identify* with that feeling. I have to: I have lowered my trust in the future, and now all there is to fill in my sense of self is this world before me, seen through my complicated eyes. The beauty I manage to find or create then seems to be beauty that finds me. It is like love, or home. You cannot help becoming the love you feel, or feeling like you belong in a place that welcomes and accepts you. The suddenly beautiful world that comes into view when I am in the aesthetic moment, this world that seems to have unwittingly folded itself into my existence, now feels like a home, like it not only tolerates the strange existence it forced on me but welcomes me and invites me to be more myself by engaging with the beauty I find and make here.

Absorbing yourself in the aesthetic present has a curious effect: it slings you back into the world. Aesthetic engagement is not passive; it is active, moving, animating—it calls on you to recreate it, respond to it, share it, imitate it, amplify it, become it, repeat it. I can hardly distinguish between falling in love with a song and wanting to share it with friends; between seeing a beautiful landscape and wanting to take a picture; between taking the perfect bite and communicating its perfection in my face, posture, and voice; between seeing beautiful clothes and imagining myself wearing them, among others. Leonard Cohen describes many of his beautiful songs as "a response to beauty": "A lot of those songs are just a response to what struck me as beauty, whatever that curious emanation from a being or an object or a situation or a landscape, you know. That had a very powerful effect on me, as it does on everyone, and I prayed to have some response to the things that were so clearly beautiful to me. And they were alive."*

The aesthetic, aesthetic value, or "beauty," as it is traditionally known, is a self-sustaining engine of life. By opening yourself up to the world's aesthetic character, you open yourself up to being moved and

---

* Quoted in *Leonard Cohen: I'm Your Man*, dir. Lian Lunson (Lionsgate Films, 2005).

shaped by your love of it. And when you are moved by beauty in this way, you reaffirm and augment the beautiful world, finding yourself and a home in it. You open your life up to being a reflection, a "repetition," of the beauty you find.

.

Why do you have to *reckon with* your encounters with the beautiful, live up to them, respond to them? What is it about *engaging with the world as aesthetic* that inspires a *repetition or amplification of the aesthetic of the world?*

Plato asked this question over 2,500 years ago. He asked because he thought that he had a kind of answer to The Question, an aesthetic answer: "Only in the contemplation of beauty is life worth living." * For Plato, beauty is what animates your full humanity, and there is a path you can follow to realize the highest beauty.

You begin by finding human bodies beautiful. You want to love and engage with them and, as Plato put, "beget beauty." In contemporary terms,

---

* Plato, *Symposium,* trans. Alexander Nehamas and Paul Woodruff (Indianapolis, IN: Hackett, 1989).

you want to make out, play around, fuck—you want your own body to be hot, sexy, and beautiful, and you want to be with other hot, sexy, and beautiful bodies. But in wanting to reckon with bodily beauty, to engage with and understand that beauty, you want to understand what makes it good. Fucking helps, but it only goes so far. After a while you notice that beautiful bodies are made beautiful by a deeper beauty: the minds, personalities, and styles that are expressed with those bodies. Then you are also moved by this deeper beauty, these beautiful minds, and you want to reckon with them, engage with them, and understand what makes them beautiful. This moves you to yet a deeper source of beauty: the ideas, values, and principles that shape those personalities and styles. Your pursuit of beauty moves you from the realm of the body to the realm of ideas, and when you go even further, Plato thinks something extraordinary happens: all of a sudden you "will catch sight of something wonderfully beautiful in its nature." You will behold *Beauty itself*, some pure form of beauty, the engagement with which "is the reason for all [your] earlier labors."

(Did I behold Beauty itself? Is that what happened to me?)

For Plato, this progression from engaging with beautiful bodies to engaging with Beauty itself is the heart of loving and valuing your life. It is what love wants, seeks, aims at. Not just to behold and be pleased by beauty but to *engage* with beauty, to let it grip and shape your life, to animate you and initiate you into the process of "giving birth in beauty," responding to beauty by giving rise to beauty anew. When beauty affects you, you recreate it. That is why the experience of the aesthetic is so often the experience of *wanting to be* the beauty you behold. For Plato, this desire is love, erōs. Love is sparked by and creative of beauty. And this is Plato's answer to the question above about why we must reckon with beauty. The reason we must reckon with beauty is that beauty is a source of love that demands more than what it has and nothing less than what it wants.*

* Alexander Nehamas develops a wonderful reading of Plato's aesthetics in "'Only in the Contemplation of Beauty Is Life Worth Living': Plato, *Symposium* 211d," *European Journal of Philosophy* 15, no. 1 (2007): 1–18. Nehamas also offers a fascinating Plato-inspired understanding of beauty in his influential book *Only a Promise of Happiness: The Place of Beauty in a World of Art* (Princeton, NJ: Princeton University Press, 2007).

This is how attending to the aesthetic moment can become the heart of your being alive, by changing not only what you are moved to do but how you are moved. It changes who you are. You are now a being animated by beauty.

The first moment of the process of "giving birth in beauty" is being able to live in the moment and find its aesthetic. To live in the aesthetic moment is to have your heart tuned to aesthetic presence. This connection between beauty and valuing and loving life begins with developing your complicated eyes. This is what gives the existential imperative to live in the moment its force. Beauty is all around you, and you have within you the capacity to find it. When beauty is missing, you can cultivate the insight and will to create it.

And when you do, when you live this way, you leave a trail of beauty in your wake, one that others looking back on your life can see and love— your sense of humor, the smell of your cooking, the music you made and shared, the landscapes you loved, and the books you wrote.

And you can apply the same aesthetic thought to those who came before you, those who brought you into this life and, hopefully, tried to give you beautiful things to love. This is how you might care for and tell stories about your ancestors, even in the face of their pain and the suffering that defined their time, that maybe they even caused or carried into their future and into your present. This aesthetic way of relating to the past is not selective mystification but insight into, engagement with, whatever beauty you can find there. And if you look with aesthetic love, you might be surprised at what you can find: her unshakeable kindness and limitless love, her courage and resilience, her sublime selflessness; his youthful idealism, his quaint sense of style and irreverent sense of humor, his quirky gifts and sometimes awkward but so, so welcome expressions of love for you.

Just as you can look to the present for its beauty, you can look into the past for your ancestors' beauty and be similarly open to it, engaged by it. You can imitate the beauty you find, share the amazing, troubling, wild, strange, incredible stories, and translate their beauty into your own, thereby shaping your present and becoming their conduits to the future. When you find beauty in your past, that beauty almost translates itself into your present, and in shaping your present, past beauty launches itself through you and with you, into a more beautiful future. Then whatever home your ancestors' beauty helps you to find in the past can also be a home you carry with you through time.

Chapter 6

THIS BEAUTY

Why does beauty spark this desire to live in sync with the aesthetic, to engage with and recreate it? You must reckon with beauty because beauty infuses life with its special value, but what is that special value? Answers to these questions would also be the beginning of an answer to The Question because this cycle of aesthetic valuing embodies a desire to be alive. Beauty does not just give you pleasure and make you feel good. It moves you; it *animates* you. Engaging with beauty, cultivating your practice of aesthetic valuing, would then keep you engaged with being alive, and your life would repeat and reflect that beauty. Then I might be able to insist, with conviction, that being alive can be beautiful enough to be worthy of replication.

Ludwig Wittgenstein said almost nothing about beauty, but one of the few things he did say is characteristically both brilliant and obscure:

> If I say A has beautiful eyes someone may ask me: what do you find beautiful about his eyes, and perhaps I shall reply: the almond shape, long eye-lashes, delicate lids. What do these eyes have in common with a gothic church that I find beautiful too? Should I say they make a similar impression on me? What if I were to say that in both cases my hand feels tempted to draw them? That at any rate would be a *narrow definition* of the beautiful.*

The beauty of an almond-shaped eye with long lashes and delicate lids has nothing in common with the beauty of a gothic church, with its pointed arches and arcades, its sharp and reaching spires.

---

* Ludwig Wittgenstein, *Culture and Value*, trans. Peter Winch, ed. G. H. Von Wright (Chicago: University of Chicago Press, 1980), 24.

Their geometries are orthogonal, their aesthetics antithetical. Yet they are both beautiful. How? To say that they make "a similar impression" is to say nothing that has not already been said: they are both beautiful. If you look to the beautiful objects themselves, you will struggle to find something in common, but when you look to *what you do in response to them*, you will notice a similarity: the hand wants to draw what the eye sees as beautiful, whether that's a gothic church, a handsome face, or a stunning landscape. Maybe you don't draw. You take a picture, write a description, linger in the space, or let it echo in memory. In response to rhythm, you move your body; the dish is delicious, so you ask for the recipe; the outfit is stunning, so you comb through your wardrobe to recreate it. You *imitate* the beautiful. Leonard Cohen prays for a response to beauty and writes a song. A poet falls in love with the color blue and returns to its surest source, producing an "imitation": "The half-circle of blinding turquoise ocean is this love's primal scene. That this blue exists makes my life a remarkable one, just to have seen it. To have seen such beautiful things. To find oneself placed in their midst. Choiceless. I returned there yesterday and stood again upon the mountain." *

But why would the imitative response to beauty amount to a *narrow definition* of the beautiful" as opposed to a complete definition or perhaps an incorrect one? If it is a good definition in part or whole, then "imitations" must figure in the nature or essence of beauty. And if that is correct, then a more complete understanding of beauty requires knowing more about the whole of aesthetic value, not just a narrow part of it. So what else, other than imitation, could fill out this "narrow" definition?

Imitation is not your only aesthetic impulse, as you can appreciate by looking more closely at the moment of imitation: your hand draws the beauty your eye sees, and then what? You share it. Let's imitate Wittgenstein:

> If I say that this is a beautiful song someone may ask me: what do you find beautiful about this song, and perhaps I shall reply: the powerful,

---

* Maggie Nelson, *Bluets* (Seattle and New York: Wave Books, 2009), 3.

nuanced, unpredictable singing, the frenetic
music and driving rhythm. What does this song
have in common with a pair of eyes that I find
beautiful too? Should I say they make a similar
impression on me? What if I were to say that in
both cases I want to share with you what seems
so beautiful?

The aesthetic impulse to share is at least as
strong as the impulse to imitate. Beauty welcomes
both. You see a film and share your reactions and
interpretations. As I decorate my house, I think of
your future visits, hoping you will love what I do.
You dress to impress; our band plays a concert; the
chef cannot wait to release the new menu. Rare
is the painter who does not want a gallery show,
the poet who doesn't try to publish, the practicing
performer who does not imagine their audience.
Beauty is what you find, create, and propagate,
either through imitation—creating a copy, another
iteration—or through distribution of the thing
itself. Elaine Scarry writes, "This impulse toward a
distribution across perceivers is, as both museums
and postcards verify, the most common response to

beauty. 'Addis is full of blossoms. Wish you were here.' 'The nightingale sang again last night. Come here as soon as you can.'" *

Scarry might say that sharing is subservient to imitation, that through it you further the forces of imitation. I lend you a copy of the novel I loved, you read it, and now its beauty resides in both of our hearts. You rushed over to hear the nightingale; you came to Addis to see the blossoms. But sharing is also bolstered by imitation; the process goes both ways. If beauty called only for imitation, then perfect copies would be the most shareable. But you share far more than perfect copies: you share your riffs and tweaks, your inspired alterations and emulations; even beautiful songs are written and shared "as a response" to nonsonic beauty. You write beautiful essays in black ink about the beauty of blue. Sharing has its own demands and goes beyond imitation in aesthetic life; there is something additionally good in it, something beauty needs and something you need to do in response to it.

---

* Elaine Scarry, *On Beauty and Being Just* (Princeton, NJ: Princeton University Press, 1999), 6.

Although they are different when it comes to beauty, sharing and imitation make a lovely pair. They complement each other. Who is that person walking down the street? Their outfit catches your eye. You love it, and you're inspired to recreate it for yourself. You take a picture and send it to a friend. Someone shared; you imitated and shared in turn. Recipes, songs, seeds, outfits, tattoos: aesthetic life is driven by cycles of imitation and sharing, sharing and imitation.

But something is missing here, some other ingredient. After all, you don't imitate and share any old aesthetic thing: you don't rock any old outfit, you don't order everything on the menu, and so many aesthetic goods you ignore. Why did that outfit inspire? Why did you share that song, play it on repeat, find that specific recipe and recreate the dish? In one way or another, you are moved to imitate and share the things that speak to you, that seem, in one way or another, to be alive with beauty in a way that makes *you* feel alive.

When you imitate and share, you express yourself. You deploy aesthetic value—through sharing, creating, imitating, displaying—as a means of self-expression in your aesthetic engagements and

interactions. You make your own sensibility concrete in sharing this beautiful thing that somehow
speaks to you in particular. You make real, present, and social your special connection to beauty
in the way you do so many things: laughing, dec-
orating, dressing, cooking, writing, speaking, and
interacting.

Wittgenstein offers a "narrow" definition of
beauty focused on imitation. Sharing and self-
expression add to imitation. Together they make
a lovely triad that gives structure to what Plato
called "begetting": beauty begets beauty through
imitation, expression, and sharing. These actions
complement each other. When you recreate that
outfit, you do so with some vision of yourself somewhere in mind. Someone shares, you are inspired,
and you imitate and share in turn. You listen to an
album and fall in love with the music. You play it
on repeat, send it to friends, go to shows, and com-
mune with other fans. The music seeps into and
articulates your identity. You read about Maggie
Nelson's *Bluets* in a philosophy book, seek it out,
read it, and immediately give it to a friend. Aesthetic
life is driven by cycles of imitation, expression, and
sharing.

Sharing and self-expression fill out this under-standing of beauty: not only do you imitate the beautiful, but you also share it and you create and deploy it as a means of self-expression. But what do these actions—imitation, sharing, and self-expression—have to do with beauty? Why is aesthetic life so bound up with these actions?

One way to approach this question is to ask how you benefit from doing these things: what do you get from your engagement with aesthetic value when you share, imitate, and self-express?

•

Let's meet Mary Oliver in her favorite place, in the forests and fields, where she has opened her com-plicated eyes, the same eyes she sees in the playful and mysterious grasshopper. Absorbed in the aes-thetic present and "harvesting" the day, her actions are imitative and expressive, and from that place she speaks, or writes as if to speak, to you, to me. She creates poetry and distills her experience, fur-thers her imitation and expression, and shares it all with her readers. The poem teems with freedom, and when she asks you what you will do with your one wild and precious life, she tries to impart that freedom to you; she reminds you that you are free, here, now, today, and that your freedom can take the form of aesthetic engagement.

You probably aren't in a field with the grass-hoppers. You are dancing late into the night with your friends, or creating music with your band, or in the middle of a beautiful barbecue or dinner party, or listening to music while driving through the countryside, or walking through the city wear-ing your new favorite summer dress. Maybe you found or created your own "field"—on the subway, in a café with your headphones on, alone in your home, deep into a book—and whatever you find there is moving you to pause, to open up, to feel, to think, to draw, to write.

I have lived enough to know this: you will spend much of your life just trying to survive, try-ing to do well for yourself, for your job or career, your family, your children, and your friends. And this struggle will force you into fixed routines and relations that work for you, that keep you healthy, safe, and sane. These routines keep your job secure, your relationships strong; they keep the bills paid, the house running, the kids learning and growing. Living this way shapes your sense of self, and your sense of self shapes this way of life. Through these routines and by committing to the values that support them, you gain precious control over your life, and without them your life would be unfocused, chaotic, erratic, unpredictable, and probably much harder. In gaining control over your life, you give form to the way you live, and you make yourself into the person who lives this way.

But as much as you need such control over your life, living this way can be stifling, boring, all too routine. With your attention and concern always oriented toward what is next—the next bill, the next promotion, the next kid, the next meal—you can feel controlled, oppressed by all the free choices you make to give your life structure and meaning.

When you feel that way, you might yearn for a break, a night out, a vacation, a really good party, time alone absorbed in music, time to work on writing or painting or to hike in the desert, special time with friends. But notice that you probably don't want just any break: you want one that has a good dose of aesthetic value. You want to eat delicious food, listen to amazing music, play an absorbing game, watch an incredible film, have fun, or find and enter that generative, creative space. Perhaps you head out to a beautiful lake, grab your skis and hit the fresh snow, or appreciate some silence. Aesthetic value focuses and renews your efforts, disengaging you from your everyday structures and strictures and landing you in the present, with its other world of value and its more immediate senses of self and other. The more aesthetic value, the better: a really beautiful dinner is more engaging than a pretty good one, and the same goes for a really fun party or an adventurous vacation. And when your actions are guided by your engagement with aesthetic value, you will be reminded that you can be animated by something other than your self-control: you can be moved by your attention to the many manifestations of the world's beauty. In this way, engaging with aesthetic value can remind you of your freedom by setting you free, giving you perspective on your life, and reinforcing or even changing the values that you work so hard realize.

Friedrich Schiller, the late-eighteenth-century playwright, poet, and philosopher, thought that you need beauty to access this freedom: "It is only through beauty that man makes his way to freedom." Schiller thinks that it is only when beauty is in your life that you can find the balance you need to be truly free, and that only beauty can give you this balance. You lack this balance when your life is all too controlled—when all you do is work, care for the family, or plan for the future, or when you think of yourself as defined entirely by your future-oriented goals, as someone striving for the next promotion, the next paycheck, the next event. And you also lack this balance when your life is out of control: when all you do is party, indulge, seek the next wild experience. Mary Oliver reminds you that your life is both wild *and* precious. Schiller agrees. Beauty calls on you to cultivate what Schiller calls your "wholeness of character" by augmenting your ability to structure and control your life with your ability to tap into the aesthetic and be free.

•

When you tap into aesthetic value and find your aesthetic freedom—imitating, sharing, expressing— you transform yourself.

By engaging with aesthetic value, you cultivate your sense of what is worth your time and atten- tion in music, poetry, humor, design, dress, cuisine; you develop a sense of what is funny, an ear, an eye, a palate. In doing so, you become more than a human being with a beating heart: you become an individual. You become a person with *your own* sense of humor, your own sense of what is good in writing and music, your own sense of dress, design, and decor, your own taste in food, your own sense of rhythm, word choice, intonation, hairstyle—and so on and on throughout almost every dimension of your life.

Individuality is special. You spend so much of your time doing what you have to do to keep your heart beating, to keep a roof over your head, food on the table, fuel in the car, or clothes on your kids. And in so many of these matters, your choices are constrained: everyone thinks that safety and shelter are good; being fed, comfortable, and warm are good; love and friendship are good; pain and murder are bad. These are matters of valuing about which you have little or no choice, and treating them as if you have a choice about their goodness or badness would be bizarre. Your date asks you what you value, and you say, "You know, so many people like friendship and hate murder—I'm just the opposite!" While some people might have special reasons to go against the grain in some of these matters, the grain is set and vivid, and you are compelled to agree. It's no wonder, then, that the goodness of safety and love, or the badness of murder, are not much discussed at the dinner table.

While your interest in these things says something about you as a human being, it says almost nothing about you as an individual. Individuality results from the exercise of choice among goods that allow choices: you love dishes with numbing and zingy Sichuan pepper; I hate them but love the sharp, floral, earthy peppers in Mexican food. I love the Abstract Expressionists; you make fun of them. You love Kawaii metal, and so do I, but our parents will never understand us. We are different individuals.

Why can you choose to value some things and not others? For some issues, it is important that people are all on the same page. Imagine the chaos that would ensue if the badness of murder, the goodness of love, and the importance of loyalty were up for debate. Society would disintegrate under the pressures of paranoia and the desperation to stay alive. But other matters do not require consensus: not much hangs on whether everyone agrees that Ye is great, Bunyan not so much. Some people love Ye, some hate him, some are indifferent—we can have fun arguing our side while life goes on. I am not saying that aesthetic consensus never matters. It matters when you and I have to live in the same house, stage a play, or put on a fashion show, but even then whatever consensus we form is not compelled, not some discovery of what must be true—it is a creative product of our combined aesthetic sensibilities and efforts. You are free to value some things rather than others because for some things it does not matter that your valuing is aligned. When nothing hangs on consensus, you can value what you want.

And valuing what you want in aesthetic life is a good thing. Consensus might not matter much in aesthetic life, but it is also good that it doesn't. What would it mean, anyway, to be aligned on aesthetic matters the way people are aligned on love, murder, and safety? No one can watch all the good films, hear all the good albums, see all the good paintings, wear all the dope sneakers. Trying to value *a lot* of all the good things would result in a superficial sensibility, a person who never learns to spend time with the work of an author, painter, designer, or architect, or with their own creations, and really connect with and understand what they are doing. And when you choose to spend your time with this, not that, and I choose to spend my time with that, not this, the result is a bunch of individuals. Imagine the world without such choice, full of blandness and uniformity, with little to imitate and share because everyone engages with roughly the same things in basically the same ways.

David Bowie, Prince, Beyoncé, Frank O'Hara, David Chang, Alice Waters, Oscar de la Renta, Maya Angelou, Kate McKinnon, Werner Herzog: these people stand out to us in part because of the time they have spent living their aesthetic lives. A person's individuality reflects their history of valuing, their time spent loving this rather than that, a reflection of their repeated choosing. You don't get a sense of humor overnight, an ear for music in a flash, an aesthetic understanding of language from a chat, or an eye for interior design by renting an apartment. Remarkable aesthetic individuals are not always famous folks or outsized personalities, but they are always people whose connection to aesthetic value is unshakable, who live their aesthetic lives with intention, focus, and love.

Doing this is not as difficult as it might seem. In fact, you already live an aesthetic life—you already are an individual who makes aesthetic decisions every day, and you have been doing this for nearly as long as you have been alive. Everyone has a long aesthetic history. Parents, siblings, cousins, friends—as soon as you were born you were presented with the aesthetic choices people around you made in dress, cuisine, music, scent, humor, decor. You were born into an aesthetic abundance, and you react, ignore, absorb, mimic, and reject the food, clothes, music, colors, stories, styles, and jokes that surround you. Of course, some people are luckier than others when it comes to the foundations of their aesthetic histories. My early aesthetic self was formed with and against meatloaf (both the food and the music), cheesy spaghetti, "Kokomo" by the Beach Boys, Methodist church hymns, John Denver, and the soundtrack to *Dances with Wolves*.

It is easy to misunderstand aesthetic life, and because of that, you can fail to recognize that you are in the middle of living your own. Aesthetic life is not about visiting museums, drinking fine wine, supporting the opera, or even making "art." It's a way of being in, responding to, and creating the world, of being and creating yourself, and of being

with others in active, productive, valuing community. Aesthetic life reimagines and recreates the very
values that anchor and govern it so that it may continue to arc and crest and surge.

We all live aesthetic lives, but we do not all live
good aesthetic lives. Individuality varies a lot for
better and worse, and just as we do not always make
the right choices in life, we do not always make the
right decisions in our aesthetic lives. Living a good
aesthetic life is not a matter of having "good taste"
as you or I might define it. Living a good aesthetic
life is, first and foremost, a matter of intention. The
question is whether you pay attention to the aesthetic life you are living, whether you consciously
seek and value aesthetic freedom and engage with
aesthetic value in ways that refine your individuality and key you into aesthetic community.

·

When you live your aesthetic life well, you distribute and create new value: you imitate, express, and
share, and when you succeed, you become genuinely funny, stylish, playful, discerning, musical,
poetic, quirky, bold, or creative. In doing so, you
augment the aesthetic value in the world by adding

to it your own beauty, thereby yourself becoming a source of imitation, expression, and sharing—keeping collective aesthetic life, *our* practice of aesthetic valuing, alive.

If engaging with and repeating beauty makes life worthy of repeating, and the result of living your aesthetic life is the invention of your individuality, then your individuality reflects your connection to the value of being alive. And herein lies the ultimate source of beauty's value: us. I can see in your eyes, in your gait, in your music, in the cadence of your voice—and you can see in mine—that we have found answers to The Question for ourselves. And in finding and reflecting those answers, we become answers for each other. When we see and value each other as individuals, we see each other in two ways at once, in general and in particular: we see that we share this existential plight, that we have this in common, and that we found our own answers and are in the process of crafting and articulating them, making them visible to each other, for each other.

Here, then, are the goods you realize when you engage with beauty and imitate, express, and share in response: freedom, individuality, *and community*.

Consider an implication of the fact that sharing, imitation, and self-expression are so central to aesthetic life: to value the aesthetic is to value the shareable, imitable, and self-expressive. And for this reason, it is also to value something bigger than yourself: good imitation requires a person or product worth imitating, someone whose actions or creations are *imitable*; good sharing requires something that is *shareable*, and someone else must be open to and accepting of the sharing; and self-expression requires an attentive, discerning, and receptive audience. Each of these actions is social. Aesthetic life teems with social life, and aesthetic valuing is an essentially *social* practice, something we create and sustain together. This is evident in many aspects of aesthetic life: imagine being the only person at a standup comedy show, the sole diner at an elaborate feast, the lone dancer in the dark, the songwriter who never imagines their audience.

The social character of aesthetic life harbors a wellspring of social emotion and action: inspiration and aspiration, generosity and gratitude, social courage, loving attention, and encouragement. And it calls on a wide range of social skills: thoughtfulness, open-mindedness, attention to detail and nuance, receptiveness and responsiveness to others—to their invitations and enticements, their needs and aesthetic offerings. To be committed to valuing beauty, to live an aesthetic life, is therefore to engage in a socioaesthetic world of admiration and exchange. It's not much of a stretch to say that to love beauty is not just to love some object or thing. It is to love each other as individuals. More precisely, it is to love a practice that is keyed into and governed by aesthetic community, a practice that hopes for the community of individuals who imitate and are worthy of imitation, who share and are open to your offerings, whose aesthetic expressions inspire.

Now notice what happens when imitation, sharing, and self-expression go well—when you do these things with the requisite aesthetic and social skill, cultivating your individuality and sparking aesthetic freedom: you become imitable, your creations shareable, your individuality inspiring. In other words, you create the conditions for and help to realize aesthetic community.

Aesthetic community exists whenever aesthetic lives are mutually supportive: when you are open to what I share and I am open to what you share; when something you do inspires something I do and vice versa; when we are aesthetically engaged, intrigued by each other's style and modes of self-expression. Our aesthetic lives can be mutually supportive when we have similar sensibilities, when we like the same writers, attend the same concerts, make the same clothes, admire the same individuals. But wholesale agreement is not necessary because we do not need to agree, or to live similar aesthetic lives, in order to value each other as individuals. Aesthetic community is often—maybe more often than not—an assorted community, welcoming of disagreement, constructive criticism, revision, and change. You might not love the drawing I produce in response to the beauty I see, but you might see something in it, have something worthwhile to say. In sharing your perspective, I might modify or refine my own, be moved to think harder about and explain what I have done and why, or think about how I might draw it if I were to draw it again.

•

When you open yourself up to aesthetic value and imitate, express, and share in response, you contribute to the aesthetic community you and I need to thrive in our aesthetic lives, and when you thrive in your aesthetic life, you hold up your answers to The Question in the form of the beauty you place at the center of your aesthetic life and so at the heart of your being alive.

Does this answer our question, then? We have to step back and take account. There is not a single question here. There are three layers of questions under consideration.

We started with The Question: why value this life that you were unwittingly given without your consent or approval? We explored this question through the power of existential imperatives, their capacity to inspire and justify the embrace and affirmation of life. When we sort through the confusions, extremes, and idiocies of these existential imperatives, we find that they share an aesthetic dimension: they all say in one way or another that you should engage with, amplify, and understand beauty, the beauty in this life, this day, this moment, this body.

And so we started to wonder about the nature of beauty. We noticed that there is something appealingly self-reproducing about aesthetic engagement.

When we do live in the aesthetic moment, when we harvest the day, or connect with the beauty of our bodies, our style, we find ourselves responding in kind, reproducing the beautiful for ourselves and for others in our actions and products. We create aesthetic community that allows aesthetic life to flourish. Why does beauty spark a desire to live for it, to engage with it, and to recreate it?

To help us think through this question, we focused on the things we do in response to beauty. We imitate, share, and express ourselves in response to it. The hand wants to draw, in its own style, the beauty the eye sees and offer it up to you. And this led to the third layer of questions: why do we imitate, share, and self-express when we engage with beauty?

Let's work our way backward through these questions.

When you engage with beauty, you imitate, share, and self-express because, by doing these things in response, you cultivate your individuality and reconnect with your aesthetic freedom in ways that create aesthetic community. By creating aesthetic community, you create a special kind of love, where you and I see, support, and value each other for the individuals we are in ways that further our aesthetic lives, thereby deepening our love for beauty and for each other. In creating the conditions for this aesthetic love, you further aesthetic life, and together we continue, deepen, and reproduce it. You read a beautiful book, write a poem in response, and share it with me. And I am inspired in turn. Someone made music—in response to what?—you heard it and shared it with your friends while cooking them a delicious meal. Someone fell in love with the beauty of philosophy and wrote a philosophical book about beauty to share with you.

Beauty sparks this desire to live for, engage with, and recreate the aesthetic because that is what it means for something to have aesthetic value: it simply *is* whatever we can use to advance our aesthetic lives, to cultivate our individuality and aesthetic freedom, and to build aesthetic community. And we are ingenious when it comes to finding sources of aesthetic value: it is endless variety, absorbing pleasure, wild fun, eerie silence, confrontation, amazing music, hilarity, emotional drama, brilliant performance, spontaneous dance, groundbreaking cuisine, inventive tattoos, experimental poetry, bold fashion.

This gives us an understanding of the aesthetic dimension of existential imperatives: living in the moment, harvesting the day, feeling at home in your action-ready body—there are ways of grasping the power of these imperatives as animating your aesthetic life, calling attention to it, reminding you that you can be a free individual and that *we* can be free together in thriving aesthetic community. And don't you need these reminders? Isn't it too easy to forget about your aesthetic freedom, to blend into the everyday, lose your grip on your individuality, and disconnect from aesthetic community?

The remaining question is the big one: why value this life that you were unwittingly given without your consent or approval?

The fact that anyone can ask this question makes me worry that no answer will be definitive. You or I might be pleased with some answer or another—maybe for you it's religion, luxury and wealth, altruistic devotion, physical fitness, activism, or absorption in family life. There are so many forms of private or personal assent to life, and all of them have the same problem: we all know the basic truth that we did not ask to be here and do not really know what this existence is. So many ways of embracing life, meaningful and important as they may be to you, sit on this murky foundation and try to mask or massage it with distractions, obfuscations, presumptions, fantasies, and distortions. I want a most sincere answer, one that should truly satisfy, and whatever answer I offer has to face The Question head-on: I need to be able to look you straight in the eye, in all of our shared existential ignorance, and give you my answer. I won't avert my eyes or look beyond you or cast you as some villain who needs no answer or pretend you aren't staring back at me. Any answer I give will necessarily resonate with and not ignore the darkness and frustration that we are born into.

All I can do is try to make sure that whatever answer I offer you is one that I hope you recognize as the sincerest answer I can give. And my answer is this: we can keep offering each other answers to The Question in the form of beauty, in the beauty you and I bring into this world, in the beauty we create for ourselves and each other, the beauty we imitate, share, and offer up. When I look you in the eye to give you this answer, I find an answer staring back at me, in the beauty I find in you also sincerely needing an answer and turning to beauty, in the smile I return in recognition, in the metaphor that comes to mind when I see your face and notice your wild grasshopper eyes.

Chapter 7

THESE PEOPLE

What do you and I become when we find the same things beautiful, when we meet in our aesthetic lives and find ourselves, if only for a moment, living together, alive together? We form a bond over the beautiful, an aesthetic community. In doing so, we affirm beauty's place in our being alive, its power to address The Question, and we proliferate it so that others might find it too and join us in being alive in this beautiful way. In this way, we can see that aesthetic life is, at its core, a practice of giving each other our best answers to The Question. We invite each other to love the blueness of the ocean, the words of a poet, the clothes of a fashion designer, the images of a photographer, the flowers, scents, landscapes, and cuisines that keep us in touch with the value of being alive. The legendary Spanish cellist and conductor Pablo Casals (1876–1973) relied on and returned the beauty of music:

> For the past 80 years I have started each day in the same manner. It is not a mechanical routine, but something essential to my daily life. I go to the piano, and I play two preludes and fugues of Bach. I cannot think of doing otherwise. It is a sort of benediction on the house. But that is not its only meaning for me. It is a rediscovery of the world of which I have the joy of being a part. It fills me with awareness of the wonder of life, with a feeling of the incredible marvel of being a human being.*

---

* Pablo Casals and Albert E. Kahn, *Joys and Sorrows: Reflections by Pablo Casals* (New York: Simon & Schuster, 1970), 17. I became aware of this passage from Kieran Setiya's interview with Raymond Gaita on Setiya's podcast *Five Questions* (season 2, June 2021).

In our aesthetic lives, through our collective aesthetic practices, we affirm, protect, repeat, and share our answers to The Question. But what are the contours of aesthetic community? So many human bonds are cheap and dirty, formed over nothing in order to exclude everything else. You're in, you're out, that's all. We like this, they like that, and *my god, aren't they terrible?** And aesthetic community in particular can look a little peculiar: we make these useless things full of strange meaning, fawn and bond over them, and encourage each other to make more. We cultivate our individualities in ways that make us look the same. Or we find beauty in such different places that we feel completely alienated from one another. One person finds daily joy and renewal in Bach's fugues; another cannot stand Baroque piano music. How do we bring each other into the right kinds of aesthetic community? What

---

* The infamous minimal group studies in social psychology appear to show that groups can form when they are told that they prefer a certain painting or shirt color (even if they don't). From this meager and illusory bond, these groups will discriminate against other groups who have been told that they prefer different paintings or colors.

can we do to prevent it from languishing? What can we do to create this community, correct it when it spoils, and ensure that it flourishes?

.

We have been using clichés as clues. We studied how we use existential imperatives to coax each other out of a certain way of living and into one that promises to be more aesthetic, more valuable in that way. And while it took some philosophical care to separate the good interpretations from the strange, distorted, and bad, our method has been useful. When we dug in and cleaned them off, they each had their own way of pointing to aesthetic life.

Perhaps there is something you can keep in mind, something you can occasionally say to yourself, to your friends, to willing strangers, to keep aesthetic life going strong. But are you stuck exchanging the existential imperatives you can find, all confusing and misused, just sitting there in the public bathrooms of popular culture? Or can you reclaim old ones or invent new ones?

There are so many still to consider: go big or go home, keep calm and carry on, stop and smell the roses, skate or die, shit or get off the pot, *amor fati*, believe in yourself, follow your dreams, follow your heart, don't be a follower.

But existential imperatives at their best are more than nuggets of wisdom or various notes on prudence. They should remind you of the value of being alive and help you tap into the dynamics of life that keep you connected to that value. They should inspire an embrace of life and move you to act in that spirit. But if the various cliché existential imperatives confuse and mislead as much as they inspire and elevate, then maybe they are better left alone. What could take their place?

•

Perhaps the most obvious thought is the aesthetic imperative: *Let there be beauty.* If beauty and the communal practices of aesthetic life keep us in touch with answers to The Question, then *let beauty exist, bring it to this life.*

Friedrich Schiller proposed this exact imperative in the mid-1790s. And despite the profound influence of Schiller's *Letters on the Aesthetic Education of Mankind*, and despite the academic, artistic, and cultural emphasis on beauty at that time, it didn't exactly catch on.* Nor did Schiller get to witness what followed after his death in 1805: an over two-hundred-year and counting shitstorm of sexist commercialism, and the continued exploitation, objectification, and oppression focused on "beauty"—especially "women's beauty." Search for "books on beauty" and you will probably not get Kant's third *Critique*, Schiller's *Letters*, or Elaine Scarry's *On Beauty and Being Just*. You will get an avalanche of books on lipstick, eye shadow, foundation, lotion, serums, and spas. These days, if *Let there be beauty* caught on, we might end up with a Sephora on every corner. (Not that I'm opposed to that, under an egalitarian makeup regime.)

Schiller thought that you could say the same thing as *Let there be beauty* with another imperative: *Let humanity exist.* Schiller thought that these

---

* Schiller's original title in German is *Briefe über die ästhetische Erziehung des Menschen*, which is often translated as *Letters on the Aesthetic Education of Mankind*, but Schiller's *Letters* have almost nothing to do with education as we think of it and almost everything do with the central role of aesthetic value in making human life in general as good as it can be. I like to think of his title in English as *Letters on the Aesthetic Upbringing of Humanity*.

imperatives say the same thing because he thought that you cannot be fully human without exercising your aesthetic freedom. You are not realizing your full humanity if you are always so rigid, habitual, and reason governed that you are closed off to the forms of openness, exchange, and community that are required for, and that create, aesthetic life. Schiller's word for aesthetic freedom is "play": "A person only plays when they are a person in the full sense of the word, and they are fully a person only when they play." For Schiller, beauty is what puts you in the state of play, engages your aesthetic freedom. So only by creating and engaging with beauty can you be truly free, fully human. That is one reason why beauty and humanity go hand in hand, but Schiller takes it further, beyond the individual: to achieve this freedom, and so this humanity, you need to be inspired, moved, engaged by other aesthetically free people living their aesthetic lives. And so, he thought, you could not realize your full humanity without collective aesthetic life and the aesthetic value that sustains it. Individual and collective freedom go hand in hand. To wish for beauty is to wish for humanity, your own and everyone else's.

But the imperative *Let humanity exist* has its own problems. Most obviously, humanity does exist, at least as a collection of human beings, the sense of "humanity" used by the Preservationist. Only when you imbue the imperative with Schiller's fascinating way of understanding humanity, as requiring aesthetic freedom, does it resonate with meaning. But the Preservationist won't hear it that way. When they hear *Let humanity exist*, they hear their own sort of affirmation: let human beings continue their existence, let life itself be preserved, *you oughta look out.*

Near the end of his *Letters*, Schiller offered a third imperative, and at a glance it is very different from the other two: *Give freedom through freedom. Freiheit zu geben durch Freiheit!* The most obvious difference is that this imperative is not an *allowing* or a *letting* but a *giving.* Give freedom. To whom? To whomever. What kind of freedom? Aesthetic freedom. How? Through your own aesthetic freedom. This freedom is given *through freedom*, so Schiller suggests that the recipient is not owed the freedom. If they were, then the giving would be required and so not fully free. What is given is given as an offering, an invitation. Also, what is offered is not a thing, not something the recipient must *take* but something they must *do*: act, freely. When this freedom is received, a kind of gift is bestowed in return on the giver: now both are free, their humanity exists, and there is beauty.

Schiller called this imperative "the fundamental law of the aesthetic state." The aesthetic state is both a state of *mind* and a state of *humanity as a whole*, a state of our living together. It is the way of the world that will exist only when you are excellent at relating to yourself and others aesthetically. This is a "fundamental" imperative because humanity cannot exist without beauty, and beauty cannot exist without aesthetic freedom. To bring this world, the "aesthetic state," into existence, and so to bring a beautiful aesthetic humanity into the world, you have to *give freedom through freedom*. You must allow yourself to be aesthetically free, and through your aesthetic freedom you must invite others into their own forms of aesthetic freedom. In other words, you have to do your part to create the conditions that allow *us* to repeatedly answer The Question in the form of beauty. You have to create the conditions for aesthetic life, for yourself and for others.*

•

One way to understand how you can create the conditions for aesthetic life is to understand how you shouldn't. There is much to understand and appreciate about aesthetic life when it goes well. But as with any practice, especially any profound social practice, it does not always go well.

Aesthetic life can be full of distortion, unhelpful antagonism, obstruction, oppression, condescension, and pointless disagreement. You can misunderstand what is imitable, share what should not be shared, express yourself in inappropriate or unintelligible ways. And aside from the many conflicts and

---

* For a comprehensive reading of Schiller's theory of aesthetic value and its connection to freedom and community, see the two-part paper I coauthored with Samantha Matherne, "Schiller on Freedom and Aesthetic Value, Part I," *British Journal of Aesthetics* 60, no. 4, 375–402, October 2020, and "Schiller on Freedom and Aesthetic Value, Part II," *British Journal of Aesthetics* 61, no. 1, 17–40, January 2021.

problems that arise in aesthetic life, some people just don't put in the work. They have muted style, little experience, zero creativity, misplaced confidence, dull sensibility, blunt discernment, and dim generosity. Or they fail to see what is good about aesthetic life or think that aesthetic value is only about their own pleasure. Maybe lots of people are like this. But that just shows how important it is to bring intention, sensitivity, and awareness to your individual and shared aesthetic life. The same is true of moral life. Some people are greedy, self-centered, mean, myopic, entitled, oppressive, and unjust. Maybe lots of people are, but that's no reason to ignore the importance of morality and justice, or to suppose that anything goes in moral and political life. So if anything does *not* go in aesthetic life, why is that? What can go wrong?

•

Aesthetic life weaves several phenomena together: the goods of individuality, aesthetic freedom, and community as well as the actions of imitation, sharing, and expression (among others) that you perform to realize those goods. You will find missteps and distortion in each of these nodes of aesthetic life.

To be aesthetically free is to engage with the world in a more open, creative, and immediately responsive way. To engage your aesthetic freedom, you have to temper your normal sense of self and be willing to step out of your everyday habits and routines. Many familiar aesthetic practices are designed to engage this freedom directly: mosh pits, improv, raves, and freestyle rapping, to name a few. And many familiar avant-garde movements have emphasized it: happenings, situationism, social practice, Dada.

But to temper, dislodge, or tweak your sense of self in the name of aesthetic freedom is not to abandon your sense of self entirely. Aesthetic freedom is always checked by firm and familiar principles of respect, dignity, and consent. You will see this when practices of aesthetic freedom break down, when the rap battle gets too personal, when the mosh pit gets too violent, or when the ravers overdose. You will also see it when people seem to presume that their aesthetic freedom is more important than the aesthetic needs of others, or when someone's aesthetic freedom is given too much power, or mistaken for a sort of aesthetic libertarianism, from the annoyingly self-absorbed mosher or the misaligned improv actor to the controversies surrounding a range of artistic displays and performances. Aesthetic freedom is communal. It is not arm-flailing fuck-the-world don't-tread-on-me freedom. It is not you against the world; it is something you do together with others to create the best world, the aesthetic world that makes the other one yours, ours. That is why Schiller phrased his imperative in social terms: *Give* freedom through freedom. Engage with beauty for yourself and for others in ways that allow yourself and others to be aesthetically free.

The way you exercise your aesthetic freedom shapes your individuality, which is a product of the choices you make to include some things rather than others in your aesthetic life. What happens when you stake your individuality on things that are not valuable? People who do so are indeed individuals because they are exercising choice in their aesthetic lives, but their individuality is built on a foundation of error. As a result, it can be more difficult to engage them in aesthetic community, to find a mutually supportive middle ground. Doing so requires an effort to see through or past their mistakes, help them make better aesthetic choices, or see those mistakes in a positive light. In some cases, it is impossible. Consider racist jokes. An individual whose sense of humor is engaged by racist jokes is making such a serious error in aesthetic (and moral) valuing that if they offer you such a joke, even a polite smile is a nonstarter. There is no good way to take up the invitation and kick off aesthetic community.

Aesthetic community is the community of mutually supportive individuals, people whose aesthetic lives fit together. People in aesthetic community support, encourage, value, and generally care about each other's aesthetic lives. But an essential part of aesthetic community is the aesthetic freedom you bring to it, your style, your creations, insights, and enticements: people in aesthetic community invite each other into spaces of aesthetic freedom, present each other with opportunities to be aesthetically free, to cultivate and explore their individuality.

Sometimes you will be in aesthetic community with a friend, with people online, or as part of a specific aesthetic practice such as sneaker design, portrait painting, or wine making, and you will lose this element of communal freedom. It can be lost in different ways. A creative writing group that starts out open and alive turns stale when one or two members speak too authoritatively and fail to open themselves up to others' views. Similar things can happen with bands, restaurants, theater groups, and avant-garde collectives. They develop rigid habits, forget to experiment, or fall prey to overly strict leadership. Aesthetic life revolts against even the most methodical and despotic aesthetic communities. When Matisse was a young fledgling painter in Paris, he revolted against the distorted aesthetic community of French academic painting, whose strict rules and narrow view of painting seemed almost designed to produce someone as defiant as Matisse. His biographer Hilary Spurling sees this rigidity as formative for Matisse: "One of the practical advantages of a rigid academic tyranny was that it fostered, in any individual strong enough to withstand it, a correspondingly powerful urge toward freedom and individuality."[*]

* Hilary Spurling, *The Unknown Matisse: A Life of Henri Matisse: The Early Years, 1869–1908* (New York: Knopf, 2005), 67.

Rigidity and authoritarianism in aesthetic community tend to stifle self-expression. Self-expression in aesthetic life is, like sharing, a matter of putting yourself out there, finding and presenting yourself as the individual you are. You discover, affirm, and even create yourself in so many aspects of the aesthetic: in beautiful clothes, in the bands you love, in the poetry you write, in the films you celebrate, in the jewelry you wear and the food you cook. But some people mistake self-expression for standing out, as if self-expression is simply a matter of being extreme or being different from everyone else. This can lead people into forms of expression and communication that are misleading, alienating, dishonest, or even dangerous. Many YOLO tragedies result from people thinking that they will be admirable or interesting only if they perform some extreme act that makes them stand out. But standing out isn't admirable in itself, and it isn't admirable if you look stupid or are dead.

Self-expression is a matter of presenting your individuality as part of collective aesthetic life. When you express yourself well, you become a source of imitation: the ways of aesthetic valuing that define

your individuality are made visible to other individuals. Imitation is a magnetic bond, a source of
inspiration, a way to anchor, proliferate, and amplify
the aesthetic goods through which aesthetic life flourishes. Whether it is brushstrokes, espresso drinks,
makeup techniques, cocktails, or hip-hop beats,
when you engage with aesthetic value, it is with an
ear to imitation.

But the relationship between imitator and imi-
tatee can get twisted in aesthetic life, and there is
a range of words you can use to talk about each
side of the distortion: poseurs, sheep, peacocks,
show-offs, gurus, and stans. Show-offs, peacocks,
and aesthetic gurus think that aesthetic life is a
one-sided affair. Others are around to praise and
admire them, their tastes and aesthetic decrees.
Poseurs, sheep, and stans fall for the trick. They
suffuse the imitative dimension of aesthetic life
with so much meaning that it tends to crowd out
or distort the other aspects of aesthetic life; they
lose their openness to the aesthetic lives of others,
engage in narrow forms of aesthetic sharing or in
predictable forms of self-expression. Aesthetic imitation is so closely connected to the need to belong,

the desire to be seen, for acceptance and approval. When someone seems to glow with aesthetic allure, you can forget about your own aesthetic freedom and individuality and sacrifice it on the altar of the beloved other.

When you add oppression to the mix—oppression along the axes of class, of gender, of race—you not only get a distortion of aesthetic life but a nefarious tool that furthers the oppression. Oppressive body images enter into and overrun the dynamics of imitation, encouraging aesthetic distortions of imitation that further the influence of the oppressive body image—the thin body, the muscular body, the white body, the smooth body. Misogyny, patriarchy, and white supremacy conspire to tweak the aesthetics of imitation toward white men. Writer Claire Vaye Watkins confesses in her essay "On Pandering" that her writing has been geared toward emulating and sharing with the white men who have unfairly dominated the literary world, and this has distorted her sense of self-expression: "I have been reenacting in my artmaking the undying pastime of my girlhood: watching boys, emulating them, trying to catch the attention of the ones who have no idea I exist. . . . Myself, I have been writing to impress old white men."*

These distortions of imitation in aesthetic life are anchored in social and political disaster, and as such they are especially pernicious and difficult, though not impossible, to counter within aesthetic forms of life—through bold expression, courageous sharing, innovative imitation, and the like. But it can help to keep aesthetic freedom and individuality in mind and seek aesthetic communities that are clearly committed to the fullness of aesthetic life. If those communities don't exist, or if they are too few and scattered, then you might take Watkins's advice and "burn this motherfucking system to the ground and build something better."

The norms of imitation, sharing, and expression place clear limits on how you can engage aesthetic community. If you think of aesthetic freedom as unrestricted, then you might be insensitive to these limits, and when that happens, you might treat something as shared or shareable when it is not. This occurs in the aesthetics of cultural appropriation,

---

* Claire Vaye Watkins, "On Pandering," *Tin House*, November 23, 2015, https://tinhouse.com/on-pandering.

the practice of inappropriately adopting elements of another culture. There are many ethical, political, and economic problems with cultural appropriation. But one of the strongest aesthetic objections to cultural appropriation is that it treats something as having aesthetic value when it does not, or as having aesthetic value that outweighs its other spiritual, ceremonial, culinary, or ethical values. When you mistreat something as aesthetic, or misunderstand its aesthetic value, you treat it as shareable, imitable, or self-expressive when it is not. In some cases, the appropriated group never aesthetically shared, wouldn't share, or at least did not share widely or with you, the appropriated aesthetic value. When you treat something as if it were aesthetically shared and shareable when it is not, you risk distorting the aesthetic community in which the aesthetic value has its power.

In 2019 IKEA started selling a "jerk chicken" dish, the global furniture giant's version of the traditional Caribbean dish of intensely spiced chicken, typically served with rice and peas. IKEA sells 150 million meatballs per year, so it is in a remarkably powerful position to distribute jerk chicken across the globe. The problem: IKEA apparently thought that "rice and peas" meant simple white rice and green garden peas. A basic search reveals the error. The dish calls for a richly flavored rice cooked with garlic, ginger, spices, and coconut milk, and the "peas" are not garden peas but kidney beans or gandules. The dish IKEA tried to share with the world was not nearly the dish that was shareable, and by calling its dish "jerk chicken," it was in a position to influence the aesthetics of jerk chicken, as people could have begun imitating and sharing the IKEA dish. People who understood Caribbean cuisine quickly called IKEA out, and IKEA apologized and stopped selling the dish. But imagine if it didn't. Imagine if it kept selling that dish and calling it "jerk chicken" to every one of its millions upon millions of annual customers. Now suppose you actually understand Caribbean cuisine and invite a friend over for jerk chicken. "Jerk chicken!" they say. "I LOVE that dish." You serve them your dish, and they glare at you: "Why did you put *beans* in the rice?" Sharing in aesthetic life requires sensitivity to the *beauty of what you share* and to the individuals with whom you are sharing.

When you forget this, you risk ruining the beauty around you and losing your grip on your answers to The Question.

Sharing in aesthetic life is second nature, but it is not always easy. Distorted communities of aesthetic exchange can make sharing more fraught than it should be by circulating the expectation that the sharer will be mocked or judged as living an inferior aesthetic life. It is tempting to defer to the haters and qualify or hedge your expression of aesthetic love, especially when something as wonderful as aesthetic community is at stake: "I know James Wood called it children's literature and not everyone likes it and I am probably dumb and basic, but . . . [deep breath] *I love the new Donna Tartt novel*," as if the first step in loving an author's book is apologizing to the haters for owning one.* But aesthetic self-respect calls for expressive courage. Sharing can be hard; sharing means sincerity, openness, vulnerability, and that is especially difficult if you are surrounded by condescending snobs, closed-minded cool kids, or wannabe connoisseurs

---

* James Woods, "The New Curiosity Shop: Donna Tartt's *The Goldfinch*," *New Yorker*, October 14, 2013.

who fail to understand a fundamental fact about aesthetic life: in the words of philosopher and film critic Matt Strohl, "Getting over oneself is a beautiful thing."* And here's the thing about sharing what you love with a full voice: it becomes a more beautiful self-expression and invites others more powerfully into your aesthetic life.

•

These distortions of aesthetic life shed light on what it means for aesthetic life to flourish and what you have to do to contribute to its flourishing. Instead of looking at distortions, let's focus on aesthetic life when it goes well, when you succeed in giving freedom through freedom, by seeing it through the lens of actions that call for aesthetic skill. The most direct way is to speak to you, to open my complicated eyes and say, with conviction and hope, *Look at this beauty*.

When I say to you, *The sunset is beautiful*, what have I done? What will you do in response? I have

---

* Strohl says this while explaining his sincere love for the *Twilight* films. See Matt Strohl, *Why It's OK to Love Bad Movies* (New York: Routledge, 2022), 107.

made a claim of sorts, even said something obvious, and you will look up, won't you, at the sunset? *Wow, it sure is*, you say, *even better than yesterday's*. But what if I said something else, something equally obvious: *That doorframe is rectangular*, or *There is a car on the road*? You might look up, but not at the door or the road. You will look up at me, eyes squinted, brow furrowed. *Huh?*

When I say that something is sleek, elegant, cute, lovely, bold, sexy, dope, fierce, or fresh, I do more than describe things. Aesthetic language is special because aesthetic community is unique. Aesthetic claims have a distinctive effect on conversation, spark a certain relation between us. Many everyday claims merely make statements, describe the world, point things out when you need to know them. The keys are on the table; the cat is on the mat. If no one needs to know about the cat, table, doorframe, or car, then random claims about them are puzzling. *Huh? Why are you pointing that out?* But if, out of nowhere, I say to you that the sunset is beautiful, you won't be puzzled in that way. Why are aesthetic claims different? Why wouldn't you respond to my claim about the beautiful sunset in a similar way? *The sunset is beautiful. Huh?*

When I say that the sunset is beautiful, I do much more than describe how things are. I invite you into aesthetic life with me, into this wonderful world of sharing, imitation, and expression. When you respond by looking up and out and saying, *Wow, it sure is*, you take up that invitation and further our aesthetic valuing. Aesthetic claims, unlike everyday descriptive ones, are invitations.

Not all invitations are good. Sunsets are public aesthetic property, obviously lovely and easy to love. So much so that it often takes a special reason to decline an aesthetic invitation to value the sunset's beauty. Imagine that your aesthetic invitation is met with silence or rebuke. You say, *That's a beautiful sunset.* I respond, *Piss off.* You would feel puzzled and hurt and wonder what reason I could have to dismiss your invitation. *Why wouldn't he want to see this beautiful sunset? I guess the light pinks blending into dusty orange and glowing peach are a little . . . mawkish.*

But what if I don't know you? What if I haven't seen you living your aesthetic life, and I can't see any clues about how you live that life? Are you into Taylor Swift, minimalism, wine, gardens, cars, heirloom corn, drag, horror films, show dogs, show tunes, or what? Absent such information, my attempts to invite you into aesthetic community can easily fail if I go for anything other than aesthetic public property. *That's a beautiful Ducati*, I say. *Huh?* you respond. *The motorcycle. Over there*, I specify. *OK*. And that's that. The goods of aesthetic community sink into the day unless you, the invitee, choose to exercise a more radical aesthetic openness.

Invitations should be designed to appeal to the invitee's style without losing the flavor of the inviter's individuality. If I think you will hate the party I'm throwing, then I won't invite you, unless I really want you to be there and know that you are a good friend who will come because I would love your presence. My aesthetic invitations should work well when I have a sense of what you love or would be open to loving, that is, when I have a sense of your individuality and what sparks your aesthetic freedom. *The new Taylor Swift album is amazing*, I say, knowing that you love Tay and inviting you into aesthetic community. You smile. *Which one?* you ask.

Maybe you don't love Taylor Swift. Maybe you even hate pop music because you have such an

intense love for what you think of as more difficult or challenging forms, or because what so many
people hear as relatable vulnerability you hear as
pandering to an unrealistically generic crowd. We
can still vibe. *The new Taylor Swift album is amazing*, I say, knowing but ignoring that you hate Swift
and inviting you into aesthetic community. *Oh,
really?* you ask, rolling your eyes with a knowing smirk. *How so?* I explain what I love, and in
my explanation you recognize my individuality. As
you respond to me with cutting insight and criti-
cal nuance, I recognize and value yours. *Sounds like
another chart-topper. You aren't bothered by her
mixed metaphors and folksy love stories?* you ask.
Sometimes, I say, *but it's crowded out by the energy
and sincerity of her delivery.* We carry on like this.

Aesthetic invitations are invitations to aesthetic
community, and we do not need to love the same
things to be in aesthetic community together. Many
of our aesthetic disagreements are not about reaching for consensus, trying to have the same opinion,
or trying to make each other more like ourselves.
They are about trying to understand, appreciate,
and value each other's individualities, exploring
the nuances in how we live our aesthetic lives and

inviting each other into forms of interaction, exploration, and discovery that help our aesthetic lives flourish.

Invitation is a skill, aesthetic connection an achievement. When an invitation is skillfully offered, with sensitivity and understanding, it creates a bond between inviter and invitee, even when our eyes don't meet. Your aesthetic invitation showed sensitivity to my individuality, to my sense of aesthetic freedom, and for that I am grateful. And when I take up your invitation, I do what you wanted, I allow you to entice me, I am willing to follow your lead. And for that you are grateful. It's a connection, an affirmation, a mutual recognition. Freedom given through freedom—it is not unlike love.

•

The exchange of aesthetic love, the pull of a little object, a vast canyon, its call to something in you and your looking over at me to say, "Look," or "Let's look."

I might hear the call in what you say and how you say it. You might see it in what I show. I might feel it when I engage with what you create, the same thing you feel when you create it. I might sense it in how I move or recognize it in how you move. When you invite me into your house and I walk into your space. When you put on that outfit and look in the mirror. When you write down the verse knowing it's just right.

Aesthetic love shines through the environments it creates and spreads its love further. Peter Schjeldahl, art critic for the *New Yorker*, writes about the experience of viewing a particular person's art collection, how it differs so much from experiencing an institution's curated collection, "where even, or especially, the greatest works feel more endorsed than valued": "It helps when the specter of a particular person, who particularly loved particular things, stands at your shoulder, urging attention, inviting argument, and marveling at the shared good luck of being so entertained."* The collector's style is woven through the works and brightens and drives your experience of them.

------

* Peter Schjeldahl, *Hot, Cold, Heavy, Light, 100 Art Writings 1988–2018* (New York: Harry N. Abrams, 2020), 27–28. Thanks to Errol Lord, who sent me the passage.

And this is how style generally works, as an expression of your aesthetic love, as revealed in the media of your aesthetic life.

•

The first moment of aesthetic community is the invitation, the claim I make, the beauty you find and share, the piece I display. You are intrigued, disturbed, moved, called: the field of aesthetic engagement and exchange opens up before us. We issue our moves in imitation, sharing, and expression. You take up the invitation and offer more in return. I see you, hear you, pay attention, and respond. Together we further our aesthetic lives. We further aesthetic life.

The space we create and inhabit when aesthetic life goes well is not the space of economic exchange, coordination, ethical aid, or work. There is exchange—this is a space we create for each other. There is mutual regard—I encounter, hear you, or see you, and you encounter, hear, or see me. It is not always easy. It is less defined, more open-ended, unpredictable, spontaneous. Interpretations are not fixed in advance or in stone. We improvise and imagine, open up our responsiveness, make it pliable and shape it to what the other offers. We do this not only in aesthetic conversation but across the spectrum of aesthetic action, playing music or dancing together, at dinner parties and festivals, critiquing each other's work, wandering through a vast museum or a fascinating city.

We play.

When you share, express, and imitate, you engage in special forms of community and love that are constantly challenged by life, which is often governed by prophetic rules, repeatable scripts, stringent laws, and generic forms. These forces will push you away from the practice of aesthetic valuing through forms of masculinity that would withhold your love from the beauty that needs it and steel you against sharing and expression; through forms of femininity that would quiet, diminish, or distort your voice; through pressures of conformity and habit that would alienate you from aesthetic freedom and play.

But in pure play, your actions are not strictly governed by rules or scripts. In play, you are not at work, and although you are full of respect for others, morality is not at the forefront of your engagement. It's in the background, keeping its singular eye on you and me. In play, we open up space that allows us to relate to each other even more freely. I present to you, and you present to me, opportunities to engage in unscripted, spontaneous, imaginative, responsive, expressive action.

And when we do, then together we inhabit the aesthetic freedom that, if anything, is our birthright, the basic shape of our being here at all. You didn't ask to be here. You didn't consent to being alive. No one spoke with you before all of this to see whether you would mind being a bounded, conscious, material thing thrust into a fleshy, delicate, short life on some spinning space orb. In some galaxy. In some universe. In some . . . place. Yet here we are. Nothing places this fact more firmly at the center of your active, engaged life than play. Play returns you to the volitional openness that is everyone's existential origin.

•

And it would be a gift, wouldn't it, to be among people who invite you to return to that primordial place and see it anew, reinhabit it, embody its freedom and, instead of obscuring it or running away from it, make it part of your life, anchoring it in

your style and your style in it in ways that you want
to share with others?

Giving freedom through freedom is a gift, and
gifts are presents, value offered unbidden, invitations to accept and connections affirmed. Maybe I
cannot make sense of the idea that life is a gift, but
aesthetic life is a gift we give each other. It is the gift
of being alive.

Maybe life itself is not some gift given from parent to child, but life has value when you engage in
giving: your openness and invitation to value, your
spontaneity and play, your reception and gratitude.
This is what a child can give to their parents. We
bring you to life, and you make us alive. If a parent says to their child that life is a gift, I think they
mean: your life is a gift to us. And since it is a gift
we need, your life is the perfect gift.

And as our gift to you, we will bring you into
beauty and help you find yourself, your home here.
We will help you imagine beyond a "you" or an
"I"—together, you and I will help you and us make
a "we" in our collective effort to be with beauty.
And we will love you, and play with you, and invite
you to notice the leaves in the wind, the cut of a
good outfit, the rhythm of a beat, the taste and feel

of a great meal together, the grasshoppers and the petals, to dance, to feel your spontaneity, to love the blueness of the ocean.

We live in uncertain anticipation of what our lives will be, in ignorance of what our lives are, unsettled by what they have been, afraid of what they could have been. Our lives are lived hemmed in by habit and hardship, out on the open planes of our days and changing bodies, among these people, this beauty. These are the things that are here with us, for us, as us, which we must look at and love, and through our love, imagination, and aesthetic action they and we can become what we need to make our existence something more than strange and endurable. We can make it beautiful.

ACKNOWLEDGMENTS

Thanks to Emma Berry for her patience, encouragement, and editorial insight. And thank you, Emma, for commiserating with me about the many challenges of pandemic parenting in the middle of our conversations about this book. Thanks to Mel Flashman for her confidence and support. Mel, you are inimitable, but literary agents would do well to try to imitate you. Eric Henney, Barry Lam, Samantha Matherne, and Matt Rohal: Thank you for your help, your insights, your sympathy. You made this book better. So many friends, students, and colleagues offered their insights, support, and encouragement: Thank you all.

I struggled to write this book during the COVID-19 pandemic. My wife was a few months pregnant

when the pandemic started. She gave birth to our
son, and we raised him in near-complete social iso-
lation for most of the first year of his life. Thank
you, Brett, for the beauty you bring into our life
together even during difficult times. As I write this,
our son is nineteen months old, and he is a joy to
be around every day. He's not talking yet, but he
knows the ASL sign for "beautiful."

INDEX

Adams, John, 127
aesthetic community, 169
  attempts to invite one
    into, 206–207
  contours of, 183
  contribution to, 173
  creation of, 175
  description of, 194
  difficulty of engaging
    others in, 193
  first moment of, 210
  freedom in, 177
  limits on engagement in,
    199
  Matisse's revolting
    against, 195
  practice keyed into, 172
  rigidity and
    authoritarianism in,
    196
  risk of distorting,
    200
  uniqueness of, 204
aesthetic freedom. *See also*
  freedom
  aesthetic community
    and, 194
  aesthetic value and, 163,
    169
  alienation from, 211
  birthright of, 212
  engagement of, 192
  finding, 163
  forgetting about, 177
  humanity and, 187,
    189
  individuality and, 206
  reconnection with, 175
  seeking, 169
  sensitivity in, 199

aesthetic imperative,
    existence of beauty,
    185
aesthetic love, 149, 176,
    202, 208
aesthetic state,
    fundamental law of
    (Schiller), 189
aesthetic value
    aesthetic freedom and,
        163, 169
    beauty as, 23–24
    benefit from engagement
        with, 159, 162
    deployment of, 157
    engagement with
        (imitation and), 197
    of film, 60
    focus of, 162
    humanity sustained by,
        187
    meaning of, 176
    mistreatment of
        something as having,
        200
    of plant, 111
    requirement
        for complete
        understanding of
        beauty, 154
    as self-sustaining engine
        of life, 144
    unshakable connection
        to, 167

Alden, John, Sr., 127
ancestors, 148–150
Angelou, Maya, 167
Aristotle, 95

Beach Boys, 168
beauty, 151–179
    aesthetic community
        (contribution to),
        173
    aesthetic freedom, 163,
        169
    aesthetic history, 168
    aesthetic impulse, 155
    aesthetic value, 23–24
    aesthetic value (benefit
        from engagement
        with), 159
    aesthetic value
        (deployment of), 157
    aesthetic value (focus
        of), 162
    aesthetic value
        (something having),
        176
    basic truth, 178
    "begetting," 158
    complete understanding
        of, 154
    engaging with, 151
    existence of (imperative),
        185
    existential imperatives,
        177

freedom (access to), 162, 163

"giving birth in," 148

grasshopper example, 159–160

imitation, 154

individuality, 164–165, 169, 172

as invitation and acceptance, 24

love of, 172

missing, 148

misunderstanding of aesthetic life, 168

of music, 182

mutually supportive aesthetic lives, 173

"narrow definition of the beautiful," 154

nature of, 174–175

profound experience of, 130

self-expression, 157–158, 159

as self-sustaining engine of life, 144

sharing (imitation and), 156, 157

social character of aesthetic life, 171

things we do in response to, 175

value creation, 169

valuing what you want in aesthetic life, 166

Beyoncé, 167

birth

as beginning of long story, 32

"giving birth in beauty," 147, 148

parents sued for giving, 3

The Question about, 14

reminder of circumstances of, 75

Bluets (Nelson), 158

body, 63–90

as abandoned temple, 64

abuse of (YOLO and), 63–64

aesthetic bodily perspective (nefarious sources of), 79

"backyard" (clinging to), 75

delicacy of, 16, 17–18

friendship and guidance (need for), 73

home, 75, 76

mantras of wellness, 89

Matisse, 80–88

movements (perspective on), 77–78

perception of, 69

preciousness, 67–68

body (*continued*)
preservation of (YOLO and), 66
Preservationist's view of, 64
pull of each side, 65
The Question (social forces and), 69
self-love (imperatives to), 65
skate park experience, 72
social pressures (bodily action and), 71–72
social world, 69
society's answers to The Question, 70
as temple, 65
Bowie, David, 167
Boy Meets World, 73
bread maker analogy, 35–36, 56
Buddhism, 132

carpe diem, 29
association of hard work with, 117, 121
command of, 95
common definitions of, 92
impulse behind, 102
interpretation of, 99
John Keating interpretation, 96–97

meaning of, 93, 96
power of, 98
trust and, 113
Casals, Pablo, 182
Chang, David, 167
Clavigo (Goethe), 27–28
Cohen, Leonard, 144, 153
Collins, Billy, 4
Critique, (Kant), 186

Dances with Wolves, 168
days, 91–123
aesthetic value, 111–112
aggressive metaphors, 101
best desires (acting on), 96
carpe diem (common definitions of), 92
carpe diem (impulse behind), 102
carpe diem (John Keating interpretation), 96–97
carpe diem (trust and), 113
existential imperatives, 102
the future, 104, 109–110, 115, 116
as homiest medium of life, 91
Horace's advice, 118

"incontinence"
(Aristotle), 95
literal seizure, 93–94
metaphoric seizure of,
93
moral rules, 102–103
plans, 121
poem, 119–120
pursuit of good things in
life, 99
The Question (answers
to), 123
The Question (being in
the grip of), 98
The Question (in
culinary form), 100
robbery incident,
106–108
as something you create,
122
ways of thinking, 101
De la Renta, Oscar, 167
Dead Poets Society, 96
death
as abstract end, 32
being close to, 16
certainty of, 58
chance of, 104
connection between
meaning and, 43
contemplation of, 40
fool's fakery about, 109
of Matisse, 87
necessity of, 41–42

profound clarity about,
129
questions about, 15
real thought of, 108
reminder of, 39
as repayment of capital,
7
of Schiller, 186
as ultimate source of
fear, 105
YOLO versus non-
YOLO, 40
Denver, John, 168
Drake, 29, 30

Eminem, 74
Empson, William, 46
eternal recurrence
Nietzsche's idea of, 51,
54
seeking of "tremendous
moment" while
contemplating, 52
you only live once and,
53
existential imperatives
aesthetic dimension of,
177
body as focus of, 65
clichéd, 92
embrace of life inspired
by, 185
examples of, 19, 104
force of, 148

existential imperatives
(*continued*)
impulse behind, 102
meaning and force
expected from, 140
power of, 55, 135, 174
problems with, 20, 92
promise of, 61
promise of embrace
lurking behind, 50
The Question not
answered by, 141
register of (to self-love),
66
useless mass of
(Thoreau), 134
work of (question of), 21

father, 8–10, 126–127,
149
Ferrari, 13
Fischer, John Martin,
135–136, 141
freedom
access to, 162, 163
in aesthetic community,
177
attempts to avoid, 59
as benefit of engaging
with beauty, 170, 175
communal, 193, 195
embracing life with, 31
giving, 188, 193, 203,
213

invitation and, 188–189
opening up of body to,
76
poem teeming with,
159
reminder of, 162
the future
dependence on, 109–110,
115, 116
existential imperative
and, 104, 109
fictional self in, 136
hopeful vision of, 128
as illusion, 132
importance of, 134
nonexistence of, 136
planning for, 163
seeing the present as,
117
trust in, 118, 122, 143
ways of disarming, 142

guitar, 34, 45-46
Goethe, 27–28

Haile Selassie, 74
Harrelson, Woody, 74
Herzog, Werner, 167
home, 75, 76
in body, 76, 87, 177
self-love as, 90
in time, 125–126, 145
in the world, 115–116
Horace, 93, 113, 114, 119

imitation
  beauty found through,
    155
  distortions of, 199
  dynamics of (oppressive
    body images and), 198
  innovative, 199
  as magnetic bond, 197
  moment of, 154
  moves issued in, 210
  "narrow" definition of
    beauty focused on,
    158
  poet's production of,
    153
  requirement of, 171
  response to beauty, 154
  sharing as
    complementary to,
    157
  subservience of sharing
    to, 156
  yourself as source of,
    170, 196
immortality, 43
individuality, 164–165,
    169
  built on foundation of
    error, 193
  cultivation of, 176
  inspiring, 172
  invention of, 170
  losing your grip on, 177
  recognition of, 207

resulting from exercise
    of choice, 165
  self-expression and,
    196
  sensitivity to, 208
  special, 164
Inkyy, 30
invitation
  aesthetic claims as, 205
  beauty as, 24
  decline of, 205
  design of, 206
  disagreements, 207
  as first moment of
    aesthetic community,
    210
  freedom and, 188–189
  sensitivity to
    individuality shown
    by, 208
  as skill, 208
  taking up, 205
irony, 49, 50
It Was Written (Nas), 74
Itami, Juzo, 52

Jew'elz, 30

Keating, John, 96–97

Lamar, Kendrick, 38
"The Lanyard" (Collins),
    4–5
Larson, Jonathan, 29

*Letters on Aesthetic
    Education of Mankind*
    Schiller), 185
Levine, Adam, 38
life, 27–62
    absurdity of, 46, 47, 49
    birth and death, 31
    bread maker, 35–36, 56
    call of the spirit, 57
    connection between
        having and embracing
        life, 36
    connection between
        meaning and death,
        43
    death, 41–42
    engagement in being
        fully alive, 59
    essay responses, 29–30
    eternal recurrence, 51,
        52, 53, 54
    finitude, 46
    homiest medium of, 91
    immortality, 43
    irony, 50
    now, 31–32
    other life, 57, 58
    plans, 32
    precious control over,
        161
    Preservationist, difficulty
        with, 44–45
    Preservationist
        Objection, 38–39

pursuit of interests, 42
The Question, 33
received unbidden
    (goodness of), 32
recent trends, 30
sadness, 46
social climbing, 28, 30
stages of, 55
unpredictable moment,
    48–49
valuing (question of),
    177
way that life seems
    special, 37
ways of thinking about,
    56
what to do now to
    embrace, 56
worthiness of
    replication, 24
YOLO, 29, 38
YOLO death versus
    non-YOLO death, 40
you only live once,
    demands of, 61
you only live once,
    influence of, 27
you only live once,
    persistence of, 30
you only live once,
    power of, 39
you only live once,
    strength of, 60
Lonely Island, 38

love
  aesthetic, 176, 202, 208,
    209
  of beauty, 172
  bodily, 61, 65
  bruised, 3
  created, 76
  of family, 18
  goodness of, 165
  home state, 128
  irony versus, 50
  Matisse's style produced
    by, 88
  musical, 46
  of one's life, 47
  parental, 4
  pent-up, 74
  of skating, 73
  source of, 64
  sparking of, 147
  trembling reality of, 2

Matisse, Henri, 80–88
  surgery performed on,
    80
  transformative loss for,
    81
  wife separated from, 80
  works created by, 83,
    87
Matthews, Dave, 74
Mayflower, 127
McKinness, Ervin, 30
McKinnon, Kate, 167

Memory of Oceania
    (Matissse), 87
Merchant, Natalie, 74
morality
  dictates of, 102
  importance of, 191
  pure play and, 211
Mullins, Priscilla, 127

Nagel, Thomas, 48, 49
Nas, 74
Nelson, Maggie, 158
New Yorker, 209
Nietzsche, Friedrich, 50,
    51, 54

Oceania, The Sea
    (Matisse), 83
Oceania, The Sky
    (Matisse), 83
Odes (Horace), 119
O'Hara, Frank, 167
Oliver, Mary, 119, 120
On Beauty and Being Just
    (Scarry), 186
One Life to Live, 28
Ophelia (Merchant), 74
origin story, 127

*The Parakeet and the
    Mermaid* (Matisse), 86
the past
  aesthetic way of relating
    to, 149

the past (*continued*)
  as illusion, 132
  nonexistence of, 136
  reflecting on, 105
  time as haunting
    shadow, 125
  wanting to change, 10
  ways of disarming, 142
people, 181–214
  aesthetic community
    (difficulty of engaging
    others in), 193
  aesthetic freedom
    (birthright of), 212
  aesthetic freedom
    (communal), 193
  aesthetic freedom (giving
    of), 188
  aesthetic freedom
    (principles and), 192
  aesthetic imperative, 185
  aesthetic state
    (fundamental law of),
    189
  cultural appropriation,
    199–200
  distortions of aesthetic
    life, 203
  existential imperatives,
    184–185
  gift of being alive, 213
  humanity (realization
    of), 187

individuality (sensitivity
  to), 208
invitation (as first
  moment of aesthetic
  community), 210
invitations (aesthetic
  claims as), 205
moral life, 191
music (beauty of), 182
self-expression,
  description of, 196
self-expression, distorted
  sense of, 198
self-expression,
  predictable forms of,
  197
sharing (difficulty of),
  202
Plato, 145, 147
preciousness, 67–68
the present
  absorption in, 138,
    140
  beauty of, 149
  clear-mindedness and,
    139
  engagement with, 143
  focusing on, 137
  as future, 117
  moment, 131–132
  trust in, 113
Preservationist Objection,
  38–39

Preservationists
  caring about
    preservation of life
    by, 59
  claim of, 66
  concern for the body by,
    61, 88
  description of, 38
  difficulty with, 44–45
  meaning of death for, 41
  recruit of, 61–62
  sense of "humanity"
    used by, 188
  understanding of
    humanity by, 188
  values that animate, 60
  view of treating the body
    well, 64
  ways of thinking about
    life, 56
Prince, 167

The Question, 1–25
  about birth, 14
  about death, 15
  aesthetic value (beauty
    as), 23–24
  answer, 15, 18, 21, 123
  beauty's power to
    address, 24, 151–152,
    178–179, 181–182
  beginning of an answer
    to, 151

  being in the grip of, 98
  birth, 14
  consent to existence, 10
  conversation with fetus,
    8–9
  in culinary form, 100
  death, 15
  debt, 7
  delicacy of body, 16,
    17–18
  existential imperatives,
    19–21, 141
  experience as answer
    to, 33
  human history and, 128
  life as a gift, 5–6
  life's beauty, 22
  offering each other
    answers to, 178
  parents, 5–6
  Plato's answer to, 145
  situation to confront, 15
  social forces and, 69
  society's answers to, 70
  thinking (ways of), 24–25
  way of being alive that
    addresses, 61
  world woken up to, 11
  wrong way to answer, 37

racist jokes, 194
Rousseau, Jean-Jacques,
  58, 59

Samberg, Andy, 38
Samuel, Raphael, 3
Saturday Night Live, 29,
    38
Savage, Randy, 73
Scarry, Elaine, 155, 156,
    186
Schaffer, Akiva, 38
Schiller, Friedrich, 162,
    185, 186
Schjeldahl, Peter, 209
Schopenhauer, Arthur, 6, 7
self-expression, 157–158,
    159
  description of, 196
  distorted sense of, 198
  full voice of, 203
  individuality and, 196
  means of, 157–158
  modes of, 173
  predictable forms of,
    197
  requirement of, 171
self-love, 61
  as home, 90
  imperatives to some
    version of, 65
  source of, 71, 76–77
sharing
  challenge of, 202
  difficulty of, 202
  full voice of, 203
  good, 171
  imitation and, 156, 157

moves issued in, 210
requirement of, 201
self-expression and, 159,
    171
subservience to
    imitation, 156
social emotion, 171
social world, 69
Spurling, Hilary, 195
Strauss, Johann, 28
Strohl, Matt, 203
"The Summer Day"
    (Oliver), 119
The Swimming Pool
    (Matisse), 86

Taccone, Jorma, 38
Tampopo (Itami), 52
Thoreau, Henry David,
    134
time, 125–150
  aesthetic present
    (engagement with),
    143
  beauty (profound
    experience of), 130
  clear-mindedness, 139
  disengagement, 141–142
  the future (importance
    of), 134
  "giving birth in beauty,"
    147, 148
  home in, 125
  love, 147

origin story, 127
the past (aesthetic way
   of relating to), 149
the present, 131–132,
   138
profound experience of
   beauty, 130
selective mystification
   (history as), 128
self-sustaining engine of
   life (beauty as), 144
truth, 129
wanting to feel
   emotions, 141
Tolstoy, Leo, 133–134
tremendous moment, 52,
   53, 54

unpredictable moment,
   48–49

Velleman, J. David, 48
Vuong, Ocean, 21, 22, 23

Waters, Alice, 167
Watkins, Claire Vaye,
   198
Watts, Alan, 132
Williams, Bernard, 41, 42
Williams, Robin, 96
Wittgenstein, Ludwig,
   152–154
Wolf, Susan, 42
Woolf, Virginia, 136

you only live once
   (YOLO), 14
annoyance of, 29
bodily abuse and, 63
bodily preservation and,
   66
command to live life at
   thought of, 35
connection between
   death and, 41, 46
days of living, 91
death (non-YOLO death
   versus), 40
demands of, 61
essay response to, 29–30
eternal recurrence of life
   and, 53
as existential imperative,
   19
as ideas influencing
   humanity, 27
as lively mediator, 43
living more than once
   versus, 55
love of life and, 31
making sense of, 135
meaning of, 20
movement by, 54, 58,
   59–60
opposite thought in
   response to, 37
persistence of, 30
perspective embracing
   the thought, 50

you only live once (YOLO)
(*continued*)
power of, 44
Preservationist Objection
and, 39
problem arising with,
45
realization of, 58
response inspired by, 48

response to thought of,
18
risk-averse song
transformed by, 38
spirit rushing in at
thought of, 33
strength of, 60
utterances of (effect of),
21

NICK RIGGLE is associate professor of philosophy at the University of San Diego. The author of *On Being Awesome: A Unified Theory of How Not to Suck* (Penguin 2017), he frequently lectures at conferences, workshops, and philosophy departments nationally and internationally. He is the author of over a dozen articles on topics in aesthetics and the philosophy of art. He lives in San Diego, California.